The Exceptional Case of Post-Bailout Portugal

This book explores the argument that Portugal has been an exception to the trend of political upheaval and electoral instability across Southern Europe following the financial crisis and the bailout period. It does so by mapping and exploring in-depth three key dimensions: the governmental arena, the party system and citizens' political attitudes.

The five chapters in this edited volume show that a number of factors combine to make Portugal not only a very stimulating case study, but also an exception within the South European panorama: the stability of its party system, and that of the mainstream parties' electoral support in particular; the quick recovery of political attitudes after the end of the bailout period (2011–2014); the absence of competitive populist challengers until 2019, despite high levels of populist attitudes amongst the citizenry; the successful and stable union between anti-austerity parties supporting the socialist government (dubbed the 'Contraption') and its adoption of an 'austerity by stealth' model. This book shows that it is possible to combine critical junctures and political stability, responsiveness and responsibility, through the study of one of the most intriguing cases in Southern Europe in the last few decades. *The Exceptional Case of Post-Bailout Portugal* will be of interest to students, researchers and scholars of Political Science and European Studies.

The chapters in this book were originally published as a special issue of the journal, *South European Society and Politics*.

Elisabetta De Giorgi is Assistant Professor at the Department of Political and Social Sciences (DiSPeS) of the University of Trieste, Italy. Her main research interests are parliaments from a comparative perspective and opposition parties. She has published several articles in national and international journals and the book *L'opposizione parlamentare in Italia. Dall'antiberlusconismo all'antipolitica* (2016). She has edited the volume *Opposition Parties in European Legislatures. Conflict or Consensus?* (2018) with Gabriella Ilonszki.

José Santana-Pereira is Assistant Professor at ISCTE-Lisbon University Institute's Department of Political Science and Public Policy, and Researcher at CIES-Lisbon University Institute, Portugal. His research focuses on issues such as media systems, media effects on public opinion, campaigns, political attitudes and voting behaviour. His work has been published in journals including *Electoral Studies, Journal of European Public Policy, Perspectives on European Politics and Society, South European Society and Politics, Swiss Political Science Review* and *International Journal of Press/Politics*.

South European Society and Politics Series

Series editors
Susannah Verney, University of Athens, Greece
Anna Bosco, University of Trieste, Italy

The parallel regime transitions of the 1970s, when Southern Europe was the vanguard of the 'third wave' of democratisation, the impact of EU membership and Europeanisation and more recently, the region's central role in the eurozone crisis have all made Southern Europe a distinctive area of interest for social science scholars. The *South European Society and Politics* book series promotes new empirical research into the domestic politics and society of South European states. The series, open to a broad range of social science approaches, offers comparative thematic volumes covering the region as a whole and on occasion, innovative single-country studies. Its geographical scope includes both 'old' and 'new' Southern Europe, defined as Italy, Greece, Portugal, Spain, Cyprus, Malta and Turkey.

The 2014 European Parliament Elections in Southern Europe
Still Second Order or Critical Contests?
Edited by Hermann Schmitt and Eftichia Teperoglou

Is Turkey De-Europeanising?
Encounters with Europe in a Candidate Country
Edited by Alper Kaliber and Senem Aydin-Düzgit

Crisis Elections, New Contenders and Government Formation
Breaking the Mould in Southern Europe
Edited by Susannah Verney and Anna Bosco

Italy Transformed
Politics, Society and Institutions at the End of the Great Recession
Edited by Martin Bull and Gianfranco Pasquino

The AKP Since Gezi Park
Moving to Regime Change in Turkey
Edited by Susannah Verney, Anna Bosco and Senem Aydin-Düzgit

The Exceptional Case of Post-Bailout Portugal
Edited by Elisabetta De Giorgi and José Santana-Pereira

For a full list of titles please visit https://www.routledge.com/South-European-Society-and-Politics/book-series/SESP

The Exceptional Case of Post-Bailout Portugal

Edited by
Elisabetta De Giorgi and José Santana-Pereira

Routledge
Taylor & Francis Group

LONDON AND NEW YORK

First published 2022
by Routledge
2 Park Square, Milton Park, Abingdon, Oxon, OX14 4RN

and by Routledge
605 Third Avenue, New York, NY 10158

Routledge is an imprint of the Taylor & Francis Group, an informa business

© 2022 Taylor & Francis

British Library Cataloguing-in-Publication Data
A catalogue record for this book is available from the British Library

ISBN13: 978-1-032-10620-5 (hbk)
ISBN13: 978-1-032-10621-2 (pbk)
ISBN13: 978-1-003-21625-4 (ebk)

DOI: 10.4324/9781003216254

Typeset in Myriad Pro
by codeMantra

Publisher's Note
The publisher accepts responsibility for any inconsistencies that may have arisen during the conversion of this book from journal articles to book chapters, namely the inclusion of journal terminology.

Disclaimer
Every effort has been made to contact copyright holders for their permission to reprint material in this book. The publishers would be grateful to hear from any copyright holder who is not here acknowledged and will undertake to rectify any errors or omissions in future editions of this book.

Contents

Citation Information

The chapters in this book were originally published in *South European Society and Politics*, volume 25, issue 2 (2020). When citing this material, please use the original page numbering for each article, as follows:

For any permission-related enquiries please visit:
http://www.tandfonline.com/page/help/permissions

Notes on Contributors

Pedro Pita Barros is the BPI | Fundação 'la Caixa' Professor of Health Economics at the Nova School of Business and Economics of the NOVA University of Lisbon, Portugal. His research focuses on health economics and on regulation and competition policy and has appeared in many academic journals.

João Cancela is Assistant Professor at NOVA FCSH, in Lisbon, and researcher at IPRI-NOVA. His main research interests are elections and comparative political behaviour.

Elisabetta De Giorgi is Assistant Professor at the Department of Political and Social Sciences (DiSPeS) of the University of Trieste, Italy. Her main research interests are parliaments from a comparative perspective and opposition parties.

Carlos Jalali is Associate Professor of Political Science at the University of Aveiro, Portugal. His research focuses on party systems, political campaigns and political institutions, with a particular emphasis on Portugal.

Marco Lisi is Associate Professor in the Department of Political Studies, Nova University of Lisbon and Researcher at IPRI-NOVA, Portugal. His research interests focus on political parties, electoral behaviour, political representation, interest groups and election campaigns.

João Moniz is PhD student at the University of Aveiro, Portugal. His doctoral thesis, entitled 'Mapping Politicization in the European Parliament: a longitudinal analysis', examines how political parties use the European Parliament to politicise the European Union and the integration process.

Catherine Moury is Associate Professor of Political Science at the NOVA University of Lisbon, Portugal. Her research focuses on comparative politics and institutional change in the European Union.

Edalina Rodrigues Sanches is Assistant Professor at ISCTE- Lisbon University Institute, Portugal. Her research interests comprise of democratisation, political institutions, parties and party systems and political behaviour in new democracies.

José Santana-Pereira is Assistant Professor at ISCTE-Lisbon University Institute's Department of Political Science and Public Policy, and Researcher at CIES-Lisbon University Institute, Portugal. His research focuses on issues such as media systems, media effects on public opinion, campaigns, political attitudes and voting behaviour.

Jayane dos Santos Maia is Research Fellow at the German Institute for Global and Area Studies, and doctoral student at the University of Hamburg, Germany. Her research focuses on local politics, multilevel party systems, political parties, and democracy, with a regional focus on Latin America.

Patrícia Silva is Assistant Professor of Political Science at the University of Aveiro, Portugal. Her main research interests are political parties, the recruitment of appointed elites, delegation processes and bureaucratic autonomy.

The Exceptional Case of Post-Bailout Portugal: A Comparative Outlook

Elisabetta De Giorgi ⓘ and José Santana-Pereira ⓘ

ABSTRACT

The analysis explores government, party system and political attitudes as dimensions revealing Portugal's exceptionalism during its post-bailout period (2015–19) vis-á-vis three other South European countries, Greece, Italy and Spain. It shows that government stability was greater in Portugal, no party system revolution took place and political trust recovered more quickly than in the other countries. In contrast, Portugal is not dissimilar from the other cases regarding the prevalence of populist attitudes, even though populist actors did not achieve electoral success before 2019. The article includes an update on political attitudes and government-opposition relations during the covid-19 pandemic and introduces the other articles in this collection.

The political landscape across Southern Europe has changed remarkably in recent years. Amidst the shockwaves created by the Great Recession, South European countries first went through a phase of electoral epidemic (Bosco & Verney 2012) as a consequence of economic recession, popular protest, and a steady erosion of support for governing parties. This was followed by a phase of government epidemic (Bosco & Verney 2016), with longer processes of government formation, new parties joining government coalitions and, in some cases, the need to repeat elections. In a nutshell, the last decade has allowed us to witness South European governments being ousted from power, critical elections questioning the structure of (more or less) consolidated party systems, and new challengers making their triumphal entrance onto the political and parliamentary stage (Hobolt & Tilley 2016; Vidal 2018).

The extant literature has devoted a considerable amount of attention to the electoral and government woes of Southern Europe and their short-term and long-term consequences.[1] More concretely, a series of scientific works have explored political changes during the so-called austerity period.[2] Within this literature, Portugal is often depicted as an exceptional case in Southern Europe, as the only country in which there was significant continuity with pre-crisis political dynamics both during and after the 2011–2014 bailout period.[3] Most of the specialised literature notes that the political changes that took place in

Greece, Italy and Spain were indeed much more profound than in Portugal.[4] However, albeit with some exceptions (e.g. Fernandes, Magalhães & Santana-Pereira 2018; De Giorgi & Cancela 2019; Lisi, Freire & Tsatsanis 2020), the specific analysis of the Portuguese case generally stops with the formation of the Socialist government led by António Costa in late 2015 and has not covered more recent developments.

This collection of articles aims to fill this gap by testing whether the main patterns of Portuguese exceptionalism endured in the post-bailout period (2015–2019) and identifying the most distinctive features. Our goal is to contribute to this body of scholarly work by offering an up-to-date and systematic analysis of the main electoral and governmental patterns in Portugal from 2015 to the legislative election of 2019 – to which we devote one specific article – and the victory of the incumbent Socialists. This in-depth analysis allows us to fully understand whether bailout and austerity were a ticking time bomb that was running a bit slow, with its political consequences only becoming visible some years later due to the inertia of the Portuguese political system, or if the post-bailout period is indeed also marked by a great deal of continuity.

In this collection of articles, we explore the argument that Portugal during its post-bailout period also presents distinct patterns vis-à-vis other South European countries: namely, Greece, which was still under a bailout until 2018; Italy which did not have a bailout; Spain which was in a post-bailout period but only had a bank (not a sovereign) bailout. The four research articles that follow show that a number of factors combine to make Portugal a stimulating case study – namely, the stability of its party system (and of the mainstream parties' electoral support in particular); the nature of the demand side of populism in the country and its mismatch with the supply side; the successful union between left-wing anti-austerity parties supporting the government, which granted António Costa's first cabinet considerable stability; and the remarkable business-as-usual nature of the 2019 election, despite the entry of three new political parties to parliament. The collection therefore offers the academic community a comprehensive analysis of these trends in the Portuguese post-bailout period.

In this introductory article, we identify and explore three dimensions in which similar patterns can be seen in three South European countries – Greece, Italy and Spain – but not in Portugal. These dimensions are related with both the dynamics of supply and demand in the electoral arena (party systems and political attitudes of the citizenry) and its output (government). South European countries have followed similar paths in all these areas since the onset of the crisis, but Portugal appears to be a deviant case in both the bailout and post-bailout scenario.

The article is organised as follows. The next three sections provide a comparative analysis of government, party systems and political attitudes in Southern Europe, with a focus on post-bailout Portugal. This analysis is enriched with literature and data focusing on the Great Recession period. Following this, we present an overview of political attitudes and the government-opposition relationship during the first phase of the covid-19 pandemic in Southern Europe, another unexpected context in which Portugal has showed a certain degree of exceptionalism. Finally, we discuss how the articles in this collection link to the discussion on Portugal's distinctiveness. The article concludes with a series of lessons learned about Portugal's exceptionalism in the post-bailout period and a brief reflection on the reasons behind this status.

Eppur (non) si muove: governmental stability in post-bailout Portugal

It is well known that the government sphere was significantly affected by the economic and political events that followed the onset of the financial crisis that shook Southern Europe from 2009. The 'political cost of the crisis, which had initially affected the national party systems, seems to have passed to the government level, shaking the process of government formation, changing the identity of incumbents and, ultimately, undermining the stability of the executives' (Bosco & Verney 2016, p. 383). Until 2015, the situation of Italy and Greece diverged significantly from that of Spain and Portugal. In fact, the governments of all four countries resigned in 2011 but, in Italy and Greece, this was followed by the alternation of several government solutions: first, a technocratic executive in Italy and a technocratic Prime Minister (PM) with a three-party cabinet in Greece (Verney & Bosco 2013), then earthquake elections leaving traditional governing parties with significantly reduced electoral support while challenger parties were successful, and, finally, a number of unstable executives.

In Greece, a short-lived coalition government led by a technocrat Prime Minister from November 2011 to May 2012 was followed by two elections in less than two months (Teperoglou & Tsatsanis 2014) and two cabinets in less than three years (Table 1). Prior to the crisis, Greece had had a long tradition of alternation in power between two parties, namely the centre right ND (Νέα Δημοκρατία – New Democracy) and the centre left PASOK (Πανελλήνιο Σοσιαλιστικό Κίνημα – Panhellenic Socialist Movement). In Italy, the Monti technocratic government lasted from late 2011 until the end of the legislature. In the February 2013 election, both the centre left and centre right coalitions ended up losing millions of voters, while a political force with no previous parliamentary experience, the M5S (Movimento 5 Stelle – Five Star Movement), secured about 25 per cent of votes (Baldini 2013). These results made the formation of a new government very difficult and eventually led to the establishment of an executive supported by a grand coalition formed by the mainstream parties that had previously been competing for power amongst themselves (Bull & Pasquino 2018). While no election was called until the end of the legislature in 2018, three cabinets alternated in office.

Table 1. Elections and governments in Southern Europe, 2011–2014 and 2015–2019.

	NUMBER OF ELECTIONS		NUMBER OF NEW GOVERNMENTS		CABINETS	INCUMBENT PARTIES
	2011–14	2015–19	2011–14	2015–19		
PORTUGAL	1	2	1	3	**Passos Coelho I** (21 June 2011–30 October 2015)	PSD, CDS-PP
					Passos Coelho II (30 October-10 November 2015)	*PSD, CDS-PP*
					Costa I (26 November 2015–26 October 2019)	PS
					Costa II (26 October 2019-)	PS
GREECE	2	3	3	4	**Papademos** (11 November 2011–16 May 2012)	PASOK, ND, LAOS
					Samaras I (20 June 2012–21 June 2013)	ND, PASOK, DIMAR
					Samaras II (24 June 2013–26 January 2015)	ND, PASOK
					Tsipras I (26 January 2015–27 August 2015)	SYRIZA, ANEL
					Tsipras II (23 September 2015–13 January 2019)	SYRIZA, ANEL
					Tsipras III (13 January 2019–8 July 2019)	SYRIZA
					Mitsotakis (8 July 2019-)	ND
SPAIN	1	4	1	3*	**Rajoy I** (21 December 2011–31 October 2016)	PP
					Rajoy II (31 October 2016–7 June 2018)	PP
					Sanchez I (7 June 2018–13 January 2020)	PSOE
					Sanchez II (13 January 2020-)	PSOE, Unidos Podemos
ITALY	1	1	3	3	**Monti** (16 November 2011–28 April 2013)	Technocratic government
					Letta (28 April 2013–21 February 2014)	PD, PdL, SC, UdC, RI
					Renzi (22 February 2014–12 December 2016)	PD, SC, NCD, UdC, RI
					Gentiloni (12 December 2016–1 June 2018)	PD, NCD, UdC
					Conte I (1 June 2018–5 September 2019)	M5S, Lega
					Conte II (5 September 2019-)	M5S, PD, LeU, IV

Source: Authors' elaboration of data from ParlGov database (Döring & Manow 2019).

Note: Party acronym meanings, by order of appearance in the table (original language name provided only for parties not mentioned in the main text):

- In Portugal, PSD – Social Democratic Party; CDS-PP – CDS-Popular Party; PS – Socialist Party.
- In Greece, ND – New Democracy; PASOK – Panhellenic Socialist Movement; DIMAR – Democratic Left; SYRIZA – Coalition of the Radical Left; ANEL – Independent Greeks.
- In Italy, PD – Democratic Party; PdL – People of Freedom (Popolo della Libertà); SC – Civic Choice (Scelta Civica); UdC – Union of the Centre (Unione di Centro); RI – Italian Radicals (Radicali Italiani); NCD – New Centre Right (Nuovo Centro Destra); M5S – Five Star Movement; LeU – Free and Equal (Liberi e Uguali); IV – Italy Alive (Italia Viva).
- In Spain, PP – Popular Party; PSOE – Spanish Socialist Worker's Party.

* There were formally two new governments in Spain in the period 2015–2019, as the second Sanchez government only formally took office in early January 2020. It was however included in the table since it was formed as a result of the election held in November 2019.

The picture in Spain and Portugal was significantly different. In both countries, the 2011 elections resulted a government that remained in power until elections were called four years later. In Spain, the government was led by the centre right mainstream PP (Partido Popular – Popular Party) of Mariano Rajoy and in Portugal by the centre right PSD (Partido Social Democrata – Social Democratic Party) of Pedro Passos Coelho (Table 1). In other words, at the government level, the Iberian peninsula had not yet been hit by the government epidemic.

In Spain, the competitive scenario started changing between 2014 and 2015 when two parties, Podemos (We Can) and Ciudadanos (Citizens), began posing a direct challenge to the mainstream political forces at the national level.[5] As a result, Spain had four general elections and three different cabinets between 2015 and 2019 (Table 1). The apparently small number of cabinets (compared to the number of elections) is explained by the fact that it was not possible to form a government after two of the four elections (December 2015 and April 2019) so the previous executives remained in office until the following electoral race. This is extraordinary data for a country that had been characterised since the 1980s by remarkable political stability, thanks to the alternation in government of the mainstream parties PP and PSOE (Partido Socialista Obrero Español – Spanish Socialist Worker's Party). The current cabinet led by Pedro Sanchez, appointed in January 2020, is the first coalition government in modern Spain.

Meanwhile, in Greece, both mainstream parties were severely punished in the January 2015 election, which was won by a previously minor opposition party, SYRIZA (Συνασπισμός Ριζοσπαστικής Αριστερά – Coalition of the Radical Left) in a demonstration of the Greek electorate's will for a 'total change in the governing paradigm' (Tsirbas 2016, p. 422). However, the newly formed coalition government between SYRIZA and the nationalist right-wing ANEL (Ανεξάρτητοι Έλληνες – Independent Greeks) did not last long. The Greeks were called back to the polls in September 2015 but, surprisingly, again SYRIZA came out as the major winner (Tsatsanis & Teperoglou 2016) and governed for the following four years.

In Italy, the tripolar party system resulting from the 2013 election was confirmed in 2018, but with a radical change in the balance of power between the three poles (De Giorgi 2018). After lengthy negotiations, M5S and Lega (League) were able to appoint one of the first cabinets[6] in Western Europe that did not include mainstream parties. But this alliance was short-lived: in August 2019, the government resigned and was replaced by cabinet led by the same PM, but supported by a different majority, made up of M5S and the centre-left PD (Partito Democratico – Democratic Party).

Therefore, Greece, Italy and Spain not only witnessed the crisis of governing parties and the alternation of a large number of government solutions between 2015 and 2019, but also the rise of challenger parties (Hobolt & Tilley 2016). The latter were initially confined to the opposition but later were able to win office by either forming or joining governments.

In Portugal, the situation was quite different. The 2015 legislative election did not result in either the unequivocal victory of the centre right governing coalition or the clear success of its main challenger, the PS. Nevertheless, unlike in Italy, Spain and Greece, neither of the two mainstream parties experienced strong defeats at the polls. In a controversial decision, the President of the Republic named the incumbent PM Passos Coelho as *formateur*, despite the evident lack of a majority in parliament. His cabinet lasted only a few weeks until a no-confidence motion was tabled and passed with the votes of the PS and the radical left parties, BE (Bloco de Esquerda – Left Bloc), PCP (Partido Comunista Português – Portuguese Communist Party) and PEV (Partido Ecologista 'Os Verdes' – Ecologist Party 'The Greens'). After a period of negotiation, the latter three parties decided to give their external support to a Socialist minority government for the first time in Portugal's history, thus implementing a governmental solution of contract parliamentarism dubbed *geringonça*, or contraption (De Giorgi & Santana-Pereira 2016). Contrary to the expectations of many, this executive lasted for an entire legislature.

The birth of the new government was due to a combination of factors: the PSD's shift to the right, which made an understanding between this party and the Socialists less likely; the desire of left-wing parties to avoid a second Passos Coelho cabinet; and PS leader António Costa's own personal agenda (Freire 2017; Freire & Santana-Pereira 2019). In turn, the government's durability is undoubtedly linked to the fact that the main protest parties were supporting the government, the absence of convincing alternatives – no new strong challenger parties and the main opposition party, PSD, led by the former PM until 2018 and then by the remarkably collaborative Rui Rio – and the fact that the Socialist government was lucky enough to preside over positive economic developments and succeeded in respecting the EU's budgetary rules (see Fernandes, Magalhães & Santana-Pereira 2018 and Moury, De Giorgi & Pita Barros in this collection of articles) whilst also largely fulfiling the interparty agreements on which it was based (De Giorgi & Cancela 2019).

Still frozen: the exceptional resilience of the Portuguese party system

One of Portugal's most striking features is its party system's resilience to the shocks created by the economic crisis, the bailout and the implementation of severe and unpopular austerity measures during the first half of the 2010s. In fact, neither the 2011 nor the 2015 general elections caused any earthquake at the party system level in terms of fragmentation (effective number of electoral and parliamentary parties; Laakso & Taagepera 1979) and innovation (strength of electoral support for new parties reaching more than 1 per cent of the vote, mergers and splits excluded; Emanuele & Chiaramonte 2018). The same cannot be said of the elections of 2012 in Greece (Teperoglou & Tsatsanis 2014), 2013 in Italy (Bull & Pasquino 2018) or 2015 in Spain (Orriols & Cordero 2016; Vidal 2018).

In the early legislative election of 2011, the incumbent PS was indeed punished, but this defeat was accompanied by an almost equivalent growth of the centre right PSD, no entry of new parties to parliament and a fairly straightforward and already tested government coalition between PSD and the conservative CDS-PP (CDS-Partido Popular – CDS-Popular Party) (Fernandes 2011; Freire & Santana-Pereira 2012; Magalhães 2012). Competition to the PS opposition continued to come from the traditional left parties, i.e. the BE and the PCP, as no significant new forces had entered the political arena, despite the high level of mobilisation before and during the so-called austerity period that followed the election. In 2015, in spite of the right-wing coalition that implemented the economic adjustment programme having lost a significant amount of votes, it still remained the first political force, and the only innovation in parliament was the entry of the animalist party PAN (Pessoas-Animais-Natureza – People-Animals-Nature), which is neither blatantly anti-system nor populist (De Giorgi & Santana-Pereira 2016; Silveira, Nina & Teixeira 2019).

In the post-bailout period, Portugal has remained an exception within the South European region in terms of party system stability. First, party system innovation has been remarkably low over the last decade, and this did not change in the post-bailout period (Figure 1). The 2019 figure is higher than the previous ones due to both the rise of two new right-wing parties, the liberal IL

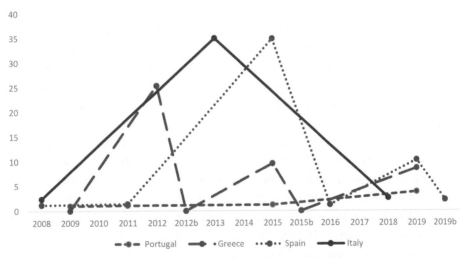

Figure 1. Party system innovation in Portugal, Greece, Spain and Italy, 2008–2019.
Source: Authors' elaboration of data by Emanuele (2016), updated in December 2019.
Notes: Figures are the percentage of votes for new parties at each election. Fringe parties (receiving less than 1 per cent of the votes) and those resulting from mergers or splits are not included. Elections presented as XXXXb are the second legislative elections taking place in that same year.

(Iniciativa Liberal – Liberal Initiative) and the radical right Chega (Enough), and the growth of left-wing Livre (Free). These three parties entered parliament for the first time, electing one MP each. Second, electoral volatility between 2015 and 2019 was quite modest in Portugal and, in fact, considerably lower than that of previous legislative elections in the country; it was also lower than that of the most recent Italian, Greek and Spanish elections, November 2019 excluded. Third, despite a slight increase in the effective number of electoral parties, no profound party system fragmentation was witnessed, especially at the parliamentary level, since it is still possible to observe a three-party system model (Table 2).

Generally speaking, none of this can be observed in the other three South European democracies under analysis. In Italy, the 2013 general elections triggered a striking level of party system innovation with six new parties entering the Italian Chamber of Deputies and occupying about one third of its seats. The most relevant novelty was, of course, M5S, an anti-establishment populist party that won the 2018 general elections (Garzia 2019; see also Chiaramonte et al. 2018; Paparo 2018), putting an end to the bipolar trend that had been established in Italy since the mid-1990s (Bull & Pasquino 2018). Interestingly, the 2018 election brought not only the growth of M5S but also a shift in the relative strength of centre right and right-wing parties, with Lega collecting many more votes than Berlusconi's Forza Italia (Forward Italy) (Chiaramonte et al. 2018; De Giorgi & Dias 2020).

In Spain, the wind of party system innovation arrived in 2015 with the electoral affirmation of two parties, Podemos and Ciudadanos, in the December general election. This was associated with a sharp decline in support for PP and, to a lesser extent, PSOE, which had already collapsed in the 2011 election (Martín & Urquizu-Sancho 2012; Orriols & Cordero 2016). These results mirror a notable crisis of representation, in which dissatisfaction with the political system as well as economic considerations led to the vote for these political forces (Vidal 2018). In April 2019, the election resulted in a second peak, albeit more modest, in the party system innovation and electoral volatility indexes, caused by the rise and entry to parliament of the radical right party Vox (Latin word for 'Voice'). This event also interrupted a long tradition among voters in post-authoritarian Spain, as it was the first time they allowed an extreme right party to enter parliament.

Lastly, in Greece, there have been three party innovation peaks over the last decade, two of them in the last five years. The May 2012 earthquake election (Teperoglou & Tsatsanis 2014) was a moment of marked electoral volatility and party system innovation. The electoral support of PASOK, hitherto a pillar of the Greek party system, was crushed in this election. Greek votes were spread across more radical political forces: on the right, the neonazi Golden Dawn (Χρυσή Αυγή) and the nationalist ANEL; on the left, SYRIZA. The levels of volatility and fragmentation declined in subsequent elections and the current Greek parliament is effectively composed of two-and-a-half parties, as in 2009–2012. However, two other peaks in

Table 2. Electoral volatility, effective number of parties, dispersion of parliamentary representation and new entries in parliament in Southern Europe (2008–2019).

Country	Election	Electoral Volatility	Effective Number of Electoral Parties	Effective Number of Parliamentary Parties	Number of Parties winning seats (new parties in parliament)	New entries (number of seats/total seats)
Portugal	2009	9.1	3.8	3.1	6 (0)	–
	2011	13.7	3.7	2.9	6 (0)	–
	2015	13.8	3.6	2.9	7 (1)	PAN (1/230)
	2019	11.3	4.4	2.9	10 (3)	Chega (1/230)
						IL (1/230)
						Livre (1/230)
Greece	2009	10.0	3.2	2.6	5 (0)	–
	2012 (May)	48.5	9.0	4.8	7 (3)	ANEL (33/300)
						DIMAR (19/300)
						XA (21/300)
	2012 (June)	18.7	5.2	3.8	7 (0)	–
	2015 (Jan.)	20.5	4.4	3.1	7 (1)	Potami (17/300)
	2015 (Sep.)	8.4	4.5	3.2	8 (0)	–
	2019	21.8	3.7	2.7	6 (2)	EL (10/300)
						MeRA25 (9/300)
Spain	2008	5.3	2.8	2.4	10 (1)	UPyD (1/350)
	2011	17	3.3	2.6	13 (0)	–
	2015	35.5	5.8	4.5	13(2)	Ciudadanos (40/350)
						Podemos (42/350)
	2016	5.5	5.0	4.2	12 (0)	–
	2019 (April)	22.9	6.1	4.9	15 (1)	Vox (24/350)
	2019 (Nov.)	11.4	6.2	4.7	20 (3)	CUP-PR (2/350)
						Más País-Equo (2/350)
						TE (1/350)

(Continued)

Table 2. (Continued).

Country	Election	Electoral Volatility	Effective Number of Electoral Parties	Effective Number of Parliamentary Parties	Number of Parties winning seats (new parties in parliament)	New entries (number of seats/total seats)
Italy	**2008**	11.3	3.8	3.1	9(1)	MAIE (1/630)
	2013	36.7	5.3	3.5	13(6)	CD (6/630)
						FdI (9/630)
						M5S (109/630)
						SEL (37/630)
						SC (39/630)
						USEI (1/630)
	2018	26.7	3.4	2.9	13(5)	Insieme (1/630)
						LeU(1/630)
						CP (2/630)
						NcI (4/630)
						+E (3/630)

Source: Authors' elaboration of data on volatility provided by Emanuele (2015), updated in December 2019; of data on the effective number of electoral and parliamentary parties provided by Gallagher (2019) and of data on new parties provided by Emanuele (2016), updated in December 2019. Official records were also consulted.

Notes: In bicameral systems, such as Italy and Spain, the data refers to the lower chamber. Party acronym meanings, by order of appearance in the table (original language name provided only for parties not mentioned in the main text):

- In Portugal: PAN – People-Animals-Nature; IL – Liberal Initiative.
- In Greece, ANEL – Independent Greeks; DIMAR – Democratic Left; XA – Golden Dawn; EL – Greek Solution (Ελληνική Λύση); Mera25 – European Realistic Disobedience Front (Μέτωπο Ευρωπαϊκής Ρεαλιστικής Ανυπακοής).
- In Spain: UPyD – Union, Progress and Democracy (Unión Progreso y Democracia); CUP-UP – Popular Unity Candidacy-For Rupture (Candidatura d'Unitat Popular-Per la Ruptura); TE – Teruel Exists (Teruel Existe).
- In Italy: MAIE – Associative Movement Italians Abroad (Movimento Associativo Italiani all'Estero); CD – Democratic Centre (Centro Democratico); FdI – Brothers of Italy; M5S – Five Star Movement; SEL – Left Ecology Freedom (Sinistra Ecologia Libertà); SC – Civic Choice (Scelta Civica); USEI – South American Union Italian Emigrants (Unione Sudamericana Emigrati Italiani); LeU – Free and Equal (Liberi e Uguali); CP – Popular Civic List (Civica Popolare); NcI – Us with Italy (Noi con l'Italia); +E – More Europe (Più Europa).

party system innovation can be observed in the case of Greece: in the January 2015 legislative election, 9.6 per cent of votes went to new parties (Rori 2016), most of them to the centre party To Potami (Το Ποτάμι – The River), and the July 2019 contest saw a similar level of innovation, leading to two new parties in parliament.

In sum, relative to its South European neighbours, Portugal is indeed exceptional when it comes to party system stability. Three factors may account for the trends observed in Portugal. The first is the lack of an innovative, alternative and credible political party and of a capable political *entrepreneur* able to exploit the citizens'/voters' disappointment when it was the right time to do so, i.e. during or just after the Great Recession and the austerity period that followed. The second factor is the choice of a significant portion of the Portuguese electorate to exit (that is, to abstain), rather than voice its discontent by going to the polls and voting for a challenger party. Last but not least, protest parties had long existed within the Portuguese parliament. In fact, this category was well represented by the radical left parties PCP and BE, which indeed obtained a very good result at the first post-bailout legislative election of 2015.

Political attitudes in Portugal: mending fences with the political system

The Portuguese case also stands apart from the other South European democracies under analysis in that, after the collapse in political support due to the economic crisis and the austerity period that followed, satisfaction with democracy and trust in political institutions recovered quickly from 2015 onwards.[7]

Satisfaction with democracy had reached manifest lows in all four South European democracies between 2012 and 2014, with average values below 2 on a 4-point scale going from 'not satisfied at all' (1) to 'very satisfied' (4) (Figure 2). However, although this indicator displayed a value of 2.1 in the four countries in spring 2015, its evolution thereafter was quite different. In fact, levels of satisfaction with democracy in Portugal rose from 2.1 in early 2015 to 2.7 in early 2017 and have not since dropped from the midpoint of the scale (2.5). The same has not happened in the other three polities. Despite a trend towards convergence among the four countries from 2018 onwards, Portuguese citizens are still ahead of their South European counterparts.

Similar trends can be seen in terms of trust in government. Again, prominent lows had been identified in all four countries between 2012 and 2014, with less than 20 per cent of citizens declaring that they tended to trust the government. What stands out again is the growth in the proportion of Portuguese citizens who trust the government in the post-bailout period. Trust levels went from 15 per cent in November 2015, during the short-lived second Passos Coelho cabinet, to 33 per cent in spring 2016, a few months after the formation of the Costa government, and 53 per cent one year later. They have not since dropped below 42 per cent. On the other hand, from 2015 onwards, the level of trust remained largely unchanged in the case of Spain, while in Italy it recovered

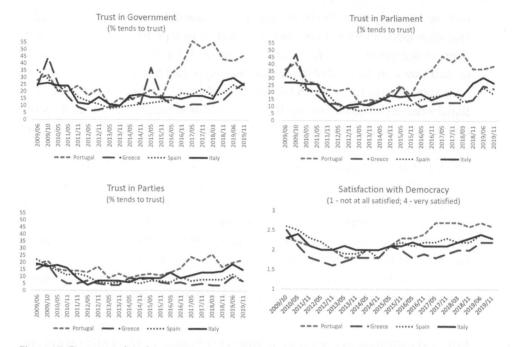

Figure 2. Trust in political institutions and satisfaction with democracy in Portugal, Spain, Greece and Italy, 2009–2019.
Source: Authors' elaboration of data from Eurobarometer.

considerably at the end of 2018, during the first months of the M5S-Lega cabinet. In Greece, after the initial enthusiasm for the new SYRIZA government in the spring of 2015, trust in government plummeted and only reached the 20 per cent threshold again in June 2019, during the campaign for an election SYRIZA was expected to lose.

A very similar story can be told for trust in parliament. Between May 2013 and 2015, less than 20 per cent of the citizens trusted the parliament in the four countries. Thereafter, a feeble recovery in this indicator is only observed in late 2018-early 2019 in the case of Spain, Italy and Greece (always with two-thirds of citizens distrusting parliament), whereas Portugal showed improvements as early as 2016, and almost half of its citizens would soon declare they trusted the parliament. Since 2018, a slight decline in this indicator in Portugal, accompanied by a positive trend in the other countries, created a pattern of convergence, but twice as many Portuguese citizens as their Spanish counterparts consider their parliament trustworthy.

The only partial exception to this trend concerns trust in political parties. Indeed, between 2017 and 2018 Portugal distanced itself from the other countries due to a positive trend in this indicator. Since then, values have dropped slightly in Portugal and improved in Italy, so Portugal does not stand out as sharply; however, in November 2019 the proportion of Portuguese citizens who trusted political parties was three times higher than in Spain and Greece.

The sudden growth in the levels of satisfaction with democracy in Portugal as of 2015 can be partly attributed to the improving economic conditions, a key factor of this attitude in contemporary Southern Europe (e.g. Quaranta & Martini 2017; Fernandes et al. 2019). Similar considerations can be made about trust in parliament, the government and political parties (Fernandes et al. 2019). Also, after the Great Recession, corruption perceptions became more important to satisfaction with democracy and trust in representative political institutions (Fernandes et al. 2019), and Portugal has scored better than the three other South European countries on this item.[8] A third possible relevant factor in Portugal is the surprising stability of the understanding between the left-wing parties, as support for a left-wing coalition (considered highly unlikely before 2015) was found to be associated with higher levels of satisfaction with democracy and political trust in 2016 (Freire & Santana-Pereira forthcoming).

Let us now shift to the analysis of populist attitudes. Over the last decade, the perception that Portugal was quite immune to the populist rise observed in other European democracies, including Italy, Spain and Greece, and the reasons underlying the resilience of the Portuguese party system to this kind of development have been the subject of debate (e.g. Santana-Pereira 2016; Carreira da Silva & Salgado 2018). To what extent is that exceptional pattern linked to differences in the demand side, namely in terms of populist attitudes? As can be seen in Figure 2, political parties do not enjoy a great deal of trust from citizens in either Portugal or the other South European democracies, even in the post-bailout period. To a certain extent, these levels of distrust can be linked with populist attitudes, at least in its subdimension of anti-elitism. But more specific data can be used to tackle this question.

Below, we present and discuss an index of populist attitudes computed from data recently gathered in Portugal (2019) and three other South European democracies (2015). This is, to our knowledge, the most recent comparable data currently available for this set of countries. The populist attitudes scale employed is composed of six statements designed to measure the main components of populism as an ideational orientation, based on the minimal definition of populism proposed by Mudde in 2004: a thin-centred ideology that considers that society is basically divided into two homogeneous and antagonistic fields – the pure people versus the elite, corrupt or incompetent – and argues that politics should be the expression of the general will, or *volonté generale*, of the people. Each of the six items, developed by Akkerman, Mudde and Zaslove (2014), provides an isolated or concomitant measure of the components of the ideational definition of populism, such as people-centrism (the people as a central element of politics), anti-elitism (a negative view of the nature and action of the elites), the homogeneity of the people and the elite, and the Manichaean antagonism between them.[9] The index was created by taking the average of the answers to the six items and varies from 0 (populist attitudes not held) to 4 (populist attitudes strongly held).

Figure 3 allows us to conclude that there are no striking differences between the Portuguese, the Italians and the Greeks in terms of how strongly they express populist views on politics. Spain scores a little lower, but still much higher than the midpoint of the scale. In general terms, levels of populist attitudes are extremely high in Southern Europe.[10] Therefore, the exceptionalism of the Portuguese case is not found in the prevalence of populist attitudes within the citizenry, which is indeed high, but in the fact that it seems that those with populist attitudes did not find populist parties or political entrepreneurs blatantly expressing these views. The leader of the new radical right populist party Chega, André Ventura (who secured one parliamentary seat in the 2019 legislative election), might appear to be the political entrepreneur figure that was lacking, but his arrival came much later than in the other countries; elsewhere, they appeared and thrived during or right after the crisis and/or the bailout. Interestingly enough, vote intentions for Ventura's party are currently much higher than the 1.3 per cent of the popular vote it received in 2019, having varied between 7 per cent and 8 per cent in December 2020 (Dinis, Garcia & Rosa 2020; Machado 2020). These polls therefore place Chega as the third or fourth most relevant political party in electoral terms. It remains to be seen if the party will be able to keep these favourable numbers until the next legislative election (expected to take place in the fall of 2023, if Costa's minority

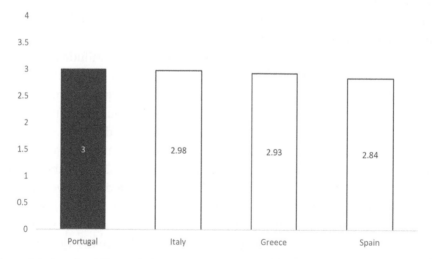

Figure 3. Index of populist attitudes in Southern Europe (2015 and 2019).
Source: Authors' elaboration of data from Sondagens ICS/ISCTE (May 2019 Report 3, available at: https://sondagens-ics-ul.iscte-iul.pt/2019/06/01/sondagem-maio-2019-para-sic-expresso-parte-3/) for the case of Portugal and from Rico and Anduiza (2019) – namely their supplementary materials online – for the other countries.
Notes: In Portugal the data was collected in April-May 2019, whereas the data was collected in the other countries in 2015. The index varies from 0 (populist attitudes not held) to 4 (populist attitudes strongly held).

government manages to serve a full mandate). If it does, that would put a definitive end to the depiction of Portugal as one of the last European democracies free of relevant radical right populist parties.

Breaking news: Portuguese exceptionalism, pandemic style

Before concluding, a few final considerations on recent developments are made in light of the exceptional times in which we live and write. As we all know, in late 2019 a new virus was identified in the Chinese city of Wuhan. The virus spread extremely quickly and an increasing number of cases of covid-19 were registered in Europe between late February and early March, with particular severity in Italy and Spain. On March 12, the Director General of the World Health Organisation (WHO) declared that 'covid-19 can be characterised as a pandemic' (WHO 2020). The consequences of this massive health emergency have touched all countries at social, economic and political levels. In Southern Europe, a range of restrictions commonly referred to as lockdowns were enforced from March to May 2020.

This first phase of the covid-19 emergency shook up attitudes towards the political system. In a recent paper, Bol et al. (2020) show that the lockdowns had a positive effect on both trust in government and satisfaction with democracy in an array of European countries. Italy is a good example of this, with one in every three citizens declaring their opinion of the PM had improved after the crisis (DG Comm 2020a). Nevertheless, a survey carried out in late April 2020 showed that trust in government was still considerably higher in Portugal than in Spain, with Italy and Greece placed in between (DG Comm 2020a).

In fact, in Spring 2020, three out of every four citizens in Portugal seemed to trust the PM's actions in the fight against covid-19 (DG Comm 2020b, 2020c). Government approval reached 60 per cent in early April 2020 – about 10 percentage points higher than in 2019 (DG Comm 2020d). May 2020 polls suggested that, if elections had been held at that time, the PS would have won new by a landslide, with a good chance of achieving the absolute majority of seats in parliament it had failed to obtain in 2019 (DG Comm 2020c).

Spain is indeed a good example of a sharp contrast to the Portuguese panorama with regard to public opinion about the government during the covid-19 outbreak. In fact, in March 2020, 36 to 43 per cent of Spaniards strongly or somewhat disapproved of the government's handling of the crisis (DG Comm 2020b). A few weeks later, 54 per cent said the government had failed more than it had succeeded, and 48 per cent had little or no trust in the way it was dealing with the emergency (DG Comm 2020e). In May, 52 per cent wanted new elections so that another government would manage the crisis, but the May 2020 polls revealed that, if elections were to be held, the Socialists would have roughly the same results they had secured in late 2019 (DG Comm 2020c, 2020f). Interestingly, citizens seemed to dislike the political struggle surrounding the emergency, since 88 per cent believed parties should support the government and leave criticism for later (DG Comm 2020e).

This brings us to another dimension that, at this time of emergency, again sets Portugal apart from other South European countries: the relationship between government and main opposition parties, and notably the behaviour adopted by the opposition in parliament vis-à-vis the executive's action. As we know, the highest level of consensus in parliament is usually found on matters of national interest commonly affecting the whole electorate (Rose 1984; Moury & De Giorgi 2015). The legislation presented by the governments to address the emergency caused by the spread of covid-19 is undoubtedly related to national interests. Nonetheless, cooperation between government and opposition was not present in all countries. To be precise, the four South European nations could be aligned on a continuum going from very adversarial to very collaborative attitudes of the opposition parties in parliament, with Portugal standing at the collaborative end of this continuum, followed by Greece, and Italy and Spain placed on the opposite side, as the most adversarial cases.

In both Italy and Spain, the opposition parties did not show any cooperation. In Italy, Lega and the far right FdI (Fratelli d'Italia – Brothers of Italy) publicly criticised the government from the outset due to the content of the measures to overcome the crisis and the fact that the executive chose to pass the emergency legislation through Prime Ministerial Decrees, without any discussion in parliament. The clash with the government peaked in mid-April, when the PM Giuseppe Conte attacked the two main opposition leaders, Matteo Salvini and Giorgia Meloni, during his TV speech to the nation (Guerzoni 2020). The Italian opposition's attitude during this time of emergency was clearly illustrated by the parade organised on the occasion of the Republic Day, 2 June, aimed primarily at demonstrating against the government (Lopapa 2020) just a few weeks after the easing of the most severe containment measures.

In Spain, despite an apparent truce at the beginning of the emergency, the government and the official opposition frequently showed signs of friction. In mid-March the PP changed its strategy and tried to turn 'the coronavirus into a new weapon of opposition to the government' (Aduriz 2020), publicly charging the executive for its actions vis-à-vis the health crisis and trying to exploit its supposed economic efficiency as compared to that of the incumbent parties.

During the Spring of 2020, the Greek opposition was generally quite supportive of the government's health measures, acting very responsibly most of the time. SYRIZA's behaviour was mixed. At first, the party supported the governmental health policies, largely because the ND cabinet relied on expert opinions before taking any of the most relevant decisions and regularly communicated them to the public (Perrigo & Hincks 2020). But SYRIZA was critical in terms of the priorities of governmental economic support (workers versus employers).

From late April onwards, Alexis Tsipras criticised the government on economic grounds, saying that its response to the crisis was tardy and insufficient.

In Portugal, the situation has been different. The PS and PSD have often cooperated with each other in the legislative process, also in hard times (De Giorgi, Moury & Ruivo 2015), and this tradition of collaboration was confirmed in the recent period of emergency. In mid-March, the PSD leader Rui Rio voted in favour of declaring a state of emergency in the wake of the pandemic and offered collaboration with the executive, which, he stated, was no longer 'a government of an opposing party, but the government of Portugal, which we all have to help in this moment' (Moitinho Oliveira 2020).[11] Between late March and April, he confirmed his position and that of his party:

> We need national unity. The country has a democratically elected government. To weaken the government is to weaken our fight. We must put aside the logic of opposition. We must all be opposed to the virus and not to each other (Avó 2020).[12]

His cooperative attitude was so striking that even the Spanish party Podemos – in government along with the PSOE – publicly noted this when it posted a video of Rio's parliamentary speech and tweeted 'This is the opposition in Portugal. So near and yet so far'.[13]

Illustrating Portuguese exceptionalism

The research articles that follow offer the academic community a thorough analysis of the patterns illustrated above in the Portuguese post-bailout period, employing recent data and adopting a comparative or longitudinal stance whenever possible and relevant, in order to permit a true understanding of the patterns of this exceptionalism.

First, Catherine Moury, Elisabetta De Giorgi and Pedro Pita Barros put forward the idea of 'austerity by stealth' as a key feature (and tool) of the 2015–2019 Socialist cabinet, and part of its success. Austerity by stealth, as they define it, means fiscal contraction that is less visible and not highlighted in the government's public speeches, and that, in the case of the first Costa government, was implicitly supported by the left-wing parties in exchange for the approval of more visible anti-austerity measures. Their argument is backed by a quantitative analysis of revenue and expenditure data (showing that although the government reverted many austerity policies, there was no inversion of the fiscal contraction in practice since the Great Recession), a case study of austerity by stealth in the health sector and several interviews with cabinet officials and MPs (Moury, de Giorgi, & Barros, 2020). Carlos Jalali, João Moniz and Patrícia Silva – while focusing on the most recent Portuguese legislative election, held in October 2019, and providing insights on the context, protagonists, campaign dynamics and events, results and government formation – argue that the first Costa government represented a weak form of contract parliamentarism:

successful in terms of stability but at the same time unable to foster enough path dependency to lead to new agreements in the aftermath of the 2019 election or to bring the left parties closer together in terms of issue positions (Jalali, Moniz, & Silva, 2020).

The two other articles focus on the patterns of continuity of the Portuguese party system and the presence of populist attitudes along with the absence of electoral success of populist parties in the country. Marco Lisi, Edalina Sanches and Jayane dos Santos Maia argue that the increasing levels of abstention on the one hand and the strategies put forward by party leaders on the other are the key factors of party system stability in Portugal. The authors demonstrate their argument by analysing the 2015 and 2019 legislative election results at the county level and reporting their qualitative research on the matter (Lisi, Sanches, & Maia, 2020). In turn, José Santana-Pereira and João Cancela focus on the demand side of populist attitudes, starting by exploring their correlates: based on an array of hypotheses focusing on factors such as socio-economic status and attitudes towards political institutions. The link between populist attitudes, electoral participation and vote choice is then explored to glean a greater understanding of whether populist citizens are less likely to vote, and, for those who do turn out to the polls, identifying their vote choices in the absence of a relevant, clear-cut, populist political party (Santana-Pereira & Cancela, 2020).

Conclusions

In the present work, we set the background for the above-mentioned collection of articles by mapping the contexts – notably, the government, party and public opinion dimensions – in which Portugal's exceptionalism is still clearly visible in the post-bailout period (2015–2019) relative to the three main South European reference cases. We confirm that Portugal presents distinct patterns vis-à-vis the other South European countries in all the aforesaid areas, demonstrating significant stability in both the input and output spheres of its political system; in contrast, the other South European countries experienced significant transformations.

In addition, while the quick recovery in satisfaction with democracy and political trust after 2015 contrasts with the patterns observed in Spain, Italy and Greece, levels of populism are similar across Southern Europe. However, unlike the latter three countries, in Portugal we find a clear mismatch between the demand and supply of populism – high levels of populist attitudes contrasted with the absence of a successful populist political party.

The patterns we observe in the Portuguese case can be explained by the lack of sophisticated political entrepreneurship, the existence of parties seen as protest parties (BE and PCP) albeit not anti-establishment, a trend towards abstention (exit) instead of vote (voice) in the citizenry, the stable relations between the minority PS cabinet and the radical left, and the fairly positive economic results. The extent to which these exceptional trends are likely to continue is surely dependent on the covid-19 pandemic management and its social, economic and political impacts. The Portuguese parties and party system have proved resilient during both the bailout and post-bailout period. It remains to be seen whether they will be able to overcome unscathed this umpteenth moment of crisis, which came only a few years after the end of the previous one.

Notes

1. Bosco & Verney 2012, 2016; Martín & Urquizu-Sancho 2012; Tsatsanis & Teperoglou 2016; Bull & Pasquino 2018; Chiaramonte et al. 2018; Orriols & Cordero 2016; Paparo 2018; Vidal 2018.
2. Bellucci, Costa Lobo & Lewis-Beck 2012; Freire et al. 2014; Moury & De Giorgi 2015; Tsatsanis, Freire & Tsirbas 2014.
3. The bailout was signed by the three Portuguese mainstream parties – the Socialist Party, the Social Democrats and the CDS-PP – in April 2011, just after the resignation of the Socialist government led by José Sócrates (who had been in office since 2005). New elections were then held in June and led to the victory of a centre right coalition which started the implementation of the Memorandum of Understanding agreed with the lenders. Portugal managed to exit the bailout programme in 2014, after one of the harshest austerity periods in the country's history.
4. Freire & Santana-Pereira 2012; Magalhães 2012; Martín & Urquizu-Sancho 2012; Tsatsanis & Teperoglou 2016; De Giorgi, Moury & Ruivo 2015.
5. While Podemos was a brand-new party (founded in 2014), Ciudadanos had been already founded in 2006 as a Catalan party.
6. There had already been a precedent, in fact, in Southern Europe represented by the SYRIZA-ANEL government in Greece, formed in 2015.
7. Quaranta & Martini 2017; Muro & Vidal 2017; Sanches, Santana-Pereira & Razzuoli 2018; Fernandes et al. 2019.
8. According to the V-DEM (Varieties of Democracy) Corruption Perception Index, available at: https://www.v-dem.net/en/.
9. The six items implemented in the 2015 survey reported by Rico and Anduiza (2019) are as follows: 1. The politicians in [country] need to follow the will of the people. 2. The people, and not politicians, should make our most important policy decisions. 3. The political differences between the elite and the people are larger than the differences among the people. 4. I would rather be represented by a citizen than by a specialised politician. 5. Elected officials talk too much and take too little action. 6. What people call "compromise", in politics is really just selling out on one's principles. The wording of the Portuguese scale sometimes differed: item 1 mentioned 'MPs' instead of 'politicians in [country]', and is therefore closer to the Akkerman, Mudde & Zaslove (2014) wording; item 4 mentioned 'professional politicians' instead of 'specialised politicians'; lastly, item 5 mentioned 'politicians' instead of 'elected officials'.
10. Based on Rico and Anduiza's (2019) data, we could also say that these figures are higher in Southern Europe than in Western Europe: in fact, countries such as Germany, Switzerland, Sweden and the UK present an average score of 2.6.
11. Quotation translated from Portuguese by the authors.
12. Quotation translated from Portuguese by the authors.

13. Tweet posted on the official account of Podemos on 7 April 2020, translated from Spanish by the authors. Tweet available at: https://twitter.com/PODEMOS/status/ 1247551332707381248.

Disclosure statement

No potential conflict of interest was reported by the author(s).

Funding

This work was supported by the Fundação para a Ciência e a Tecnologia's R&D Unit Strategic Financing UID/SOC/03126/2019 and the project IF/00926/2015.

ORCID

Elisabetta De Giorgi ⓘ http://orcid.org/0000-0002-6553-341X
José Santana-Pereira ⓘ http://orcid.org/0000-0002-1713-3710

References

Aduriz, I. (2020) 'El PP convierte el coronavirus en una nueva arma de oposición al Gobierno', *El Diario*, 10 March, available online at: https://www.eldiario.es/politica/PP-convierte-coronavirus-oposicion-Gobierno_0_1004050173.html

Akkerman, A., Mudde, C. & Zaslove, A. (2014) 'How populist are the people? Measuring populist attitudes in voters', *Comparative Political Studies*, vol. 47, no. 9, pp. 1324–1353.

Avó, C. (2020) 'Rui Rio: "O governo que vier será de salvação nacional"', *Diário de Notícias*, 29 March, available online at: https://www.dn.pt/poder/rui-rio-o-governo-que-vier-sera-de-salvacao-nacional-12003089.html

Baldini, G. (2013) 'Don't count your chickens before they're hatched: the 2013 Italian parliamentary and presidential elections", *South European Society and Politics*, vol. 18, no. 4, pp. 473–497.

Bellucci, P., Costa Lobo, M. & Lewis-Beck, M. S. (2012) 'Economic crisis and elections: the European periphery', *Electoral Studies*, vol. 31, pp. 469–471.

Bol, D., Giani, M., Blais, A. & Loewen, P. J. (2020) 'The effect of covid-19 lockdowns on political support: some good news for democracy?' *QPE Working Paper 2020-1* (Version 3), 18 April.

Bosco, A. & Verney, S. (2012) 'Electoral epidemic: the political cost of economic crisis in Southern Europe, 2010–11', *South European Society and Politics*, vol. 17, no. 2, pp. 129–154.

Bosco, A. & Verney, S. (2016) 'From electoral epidemic to government epidemic: the next level of the crisis in Southern Europe', *South European Society and Politics*, vol. 21, no. 4, pp. 383–406.

Bull, M. & Pasquino, G. (2018) 'Italian politics in an era of recession: the end of bipolarism?', *South European Society and Politics*, vol. 23, no. 1, pp. 1–12.

Carreira da Silva, F. & Salgado, S. (2018) 'Why no populism in Portugal?', in *Changing Societies: Legacies and Challenges – Citizenship in Crisis*, eds M. Costa Lobo, F. Carreira da Silva & J. P. Zúquete, ICS, Lisbon, pp. 249–268.

Chiaramonte, A., Emanuele, V., Maggini, N. & Paparo, A. (2018) 'Populist success in a hung parliament: the 2018 general election in Italy', *South European Society and Politics*, vol. 23, no. 4, pp. 479–501.

De Giorgi, E. (2018) 'The never-ending transformation of the Italian party system', in *Party System Change, the European Crisis and the State of Democracy*, eds M. Lisi, Routledge, London, pp. 155–170.

De Giorgi, E. & Cancela, J. (2019) 'The Portuguese radical left parties supporting government: from policy-takers to policymakers?', *Government and Opposition*, pp. 1–20. advanced online publication.

De Giorgi, E. & Dias, A. (2020) 'Divided, but not by much: the parties of the centre right between government and opposition', *Contemporary Italian Politics*, vol. 12, pp. 169–181. advanced online publication.

De Giorgi, E., Moury, C. & Ruivo, J. P. (2015) 'Incumbents, opposition and international lenders: governing Portugal in times of crisis', *The Journal of Legislative Studies*, vol. 21, no. 1, pp. 54–74.

De Giorgi, E. & Santana-Pereira, J. (2016) 'The 2015 Portuguese legislative election: widening the coalitional space and bringing the extreme left in', *South European Society and Politics*, vol. 21, no. 4, pp. 451–468.

DG Comm (2020a) 'Public opinion monitoring at a glance in the time of covid-19', 5 May, available online at: https://www.europarl.europa.eu/at-your-service/pt/be-heard/eurobarometer/public-opinion-in-the-time-of-covid-19

DG Comm (2020b) 'Public opinion monitoring at a glance in the time of covid-19', 20–27 March, available online at: https://www.europarl.europa.eu/at-your-service/pt/be-heard/eurobarometer/public-opinion-in-the-time-of-covid-19

DG Comm (2020c) 'Public opinion monitoring at a glance in the time of covid-19,' 27 May, available online at: https://www.europarl.europa.eu/at-your-service/pt/be-heard/eurobarometer/public-opinion-in-the-time-of-covid-19

DG Comm (2020d) 'Public opinion monitoring at a glance in the time of covid-19', 3 April, available online at: https://www.europarl.europa.eu/at-your-service/pt/be-heard/eurobarometer/public-opinion-in-the-time-of-covid-19

DG Comm (2020e) 'Public opinion monitoring at a glance in the time of covid-19', 27 April, available online at: https://www.europarl.europa.eu/at-your-service/pt/be-heard/eurobarometer/public-opinion-in-the-time-of-covid-19

DG Comm (2020f) 'Public opinion monitoring at a glance in the time of covid-19', 12 May, available online at: https://www.europarl.europa.eu/at-your-service/pt/be-heard/eurobarometer/public-opinion-in-the-time-of-covid-19

Dinis, D., Garcia, F. & Rosa, S. M. (2020) 'Sondagem Expresso-SIC: PS vale mais que toda a direita junta, PSD e Rio a descer', Expresso, 17 December, available online at: https://expresso.pt/politica/2020-12-17-Sondagem-Expresso-SIC-PS-vale-mais-que-toda-a-direita-junta-PSD-e-Rio-a-descer

Döring, H. & Manow, P. (2019) 'Parliaments and governments database (ParlGov): information on parties, elections and cabinets in modern democracies. Development version,' available online at: http://www.parlgov.org/

Emanuele, V. (2015) *Dataset of Electoral Volatility and Its Internal Components in Western Europe (1945–2015)*, Italian Center for Electoral Studies, Rome.

Emanuele, V. (2016) *Dataset of New Parties and Party System Innovation in Western Europe since 1945*, Italian Center for Electoral Studies, Rome.

Emanuele, V. & Chiaramonte, A. (2018) 'A growing impact of new parties: myth or reality? Party system innovation in Western Europe after 1945', *Party Politics*, vol. 24, no. 5, pp. 475–487.

Fernandes, J. M. (2011) 'The 2011 Portuguese election: looking for a way out', *West European Politics*, vol. 34, no. 6, pp. 1296–1303.

Fernandes, J. M., Magalhães, P. C. & Santana-Pereira, J. (2018) 'Portugal's leftist government: from sick man to poster boy?', *South European Society and Politics*, vol. 23, no. 4, pp. 503–524.

Fernandes, T., Cancela, J., Sanches, E. & Santana-Pereira, J. (2019) *Instituições e Qualidade da Democracia: Cultura Política na Europa do Sul*, FFMS, Lisbon.

Freire, A. (2017) *Para lá da «Geringonça»: O Governo de Esquerdas em Portugal e na Europa*, Contraponto, Lisbon.

Freire, A., Lisi, M., Andreadis, I. & Leite Viegas, J. M. (2014) 'Political representation in bailed-out Southern Europe: Greece and Portugal compared', *South European Society and Politics*, vol. 19, no. 4, pp. 413–433.

Freire, A. & Santana-Pereira, J. (2012) 'Portugal, 2011: the victory of the neoliberal right, the defeat of the left', *Portuguese Journal of Social Sciences*, vol. 11, no. 2, pp. 179–187.

Freire, A. & Santana-Pereira, J. (2019) 'The President's dilemma: the Portuguese semi-presidential system in times of crisis (2011–16)', *International Journal of Iberian Studies*, vol. 32, no. 3, pp. 117–135.

Freire, A. & Santana-Pereira, J. (forthcoming) 'Des politiques d'austérité et de la crise démocratique, à la sortie de l'austérité et au renouveau démocratique? Le cas portugais 2008-2016', in *L'Espagne et le Portugal Après la Crise: La Péninsule Ibérique en Transition?* eds A. Fernandez Garcia, Presses Universitaires de France, Paris.

Gallagher, M. (2019) 'Election indices dataset', available online at: http://www.tcd.ie/Political_Science/people/michael_gallagher/ElSystems/index.php

Garzia, D. (2019) 'The Italian election of 2018 and the first populist government of Western Europe', *West European Politics*, vol. 42, no. 3, pp. 670–680.

Guerzoni, M. (2020) 'Coronavirus, l'attacco di Conte (stanco e arrabbiato) in diretta tv: «Salvini e Meloni dicono falsità»', *Corriere della Sera*, 11 April, available online at: https://www.corriere.it/politica/20_aprile_11/coronavirus-show-premier-conte-diretta-tv-salvini-meloni-dicono-falsita-9396558e-7b67-11ea-afc6-fad772b88c99.shtml

Hobolt, S. B. & Tilley, J. (2016) 'Fleeing the centre: the rise of challenger parties in the aftermath of the euro crisis', *West European Politics*, vol. 39, no. 5, pp. 971–991.

Jalali, J., Silva, P. & Moniz, J. (2020). 'In the shadow of the Contraption? The 2019 Portuguese legislative elections', *South European Society and Politics*, vol. 25, no. 2, pp. 231–256.

Laakso, M. & Taagepera, R. (1979) '"Effective" number of parties: a measure with application to west Europe', *Comparative Political Studies*, vol. 12, no. 1, pp. 3–27.

Lisi, M., Freire, A. & Tsatsanis, M. (eds) (2020) *Political Representation and Citizenship in Portugal: From Crisis to Renewal?* Lexington Books, Lanham.

Lisi, M., Sanches, E. R., & dos Santos Maia, J. (2020). 'Party system renewal or business as usual? Continuity and change in post-bailout Portugal', *South European Society and Politics*, vol. 25, no. 2, pp. 181–205.

Lopapa, C. (2020) '2 Giugno, centrodestra in piazza senza regole: saltano i distanziamenti, il flash mob degenera in ressa', *La Repubblica*, 2 June, available online at: https://www.repubblica.it/politica/2020/06/02/news/2_giugno_manifestazione_centrodestra-258244031/

Machado, A. (2020) 'Chega passa a terceira força com PS mais distante do PSD', Jornal de Negócios, 21 December, available online at: https://www.jornaldenegocios.pt/economia/detalhe/chega-passa-a-terceira-forca-com-ps-mais-distante-do-psd

Magalhães, P. C. (2012) 'After the bailout: responsibility, policy, and valence in the Portuguese legislative election of June 2011', *South European Society and Politics*, vol. 17, no. 2, pp. 309–327.

Martín, I. & Urquizu-Sancho, I. (2012) 'The 2011 general election in Spain: the collapse of the Socialist Party', *South European Society and Politics*, vol. 17, no. 2, pp. 347–363.

Moitinho Oliveira, M. (2020) 'É possível fazer oposição em "tempo de guerra"?', *Público*, 23 March, available online at: https://www.publico.pt/2020/03/23/politica/noticia/possivel-oposicao-tempo-guerra-1908934

Moury, C. & De Giorgi, E. (2015) 'Introduction: conflict and consensus in parliament during the economic crisis', *The Journal of Legislative Studies*, vol. 21, no. 1, pp. 1–13.

Moury, C., De Giorgi, E. & Barros, P. P. (2020). 'How to combine public spending with fiscal rigour? "Austerity by steath" in post-bailout Portugal (2015–2019)', *South European Society and Politics*, vol. 25, no. 2, pp. 151–180.

Mudde, C. (2004) 'The populist zeitgeist', *Government and Opposition*, vol. 39, no. 4, pp. 541–563.

Muro, D. & Vidal, G. (2017) 'Political mistrust in southern Europe since the Great Recession', *Mediterranean Politics*, vol. 22, no. 2, pp. 197–217.

Orriols, L. & Cordero, G. (2016) 'The breakdown of the Spanish two-party system: the upsurge of Podemos and Ciudadanos in the 2015 general election', *South European Society and Politics*, vol. 21, no. 4, pp. 339–357.

Paparo, A. (2018) 'Challenger's delight: the success of M5S and Lega in the 2018 Italian general election', *Italian Political Science*, vol. 13, no. 1, pp. 63–81.

Perrigo, B. & Hincks, J. (2020) 'Greece has an elderly population and a fragile economy. How has it escaped the worst of the coronavirus so far?', *TIME*, 23 April, available online at: https://time.com/5824836/greece-coronavirus/

Quaranta, M. & Martini, S. (2017) 'Easy come, easy go? Economic performance and satisfaction with democracy in Southern Europe in the last three decades', *Social Indicators Research*, vol. 131, no. 2, pp. 659–680.

Rico, G. & Anduiza, E. (2019) 'Economic correlates of populist attitudes: an analysis of nine European countries in the aftermath of the Great Recession', *Acta Politica*, vol. 54, no. 3, pp. 371–397.

Rori, L. (2016) 'The 2015 Greek parliamentary elections: from great expectations to no expectations', *West European Politics*, vol. 39, no. 6, pp. 1323–1343.

Rose, R. (1984) *Do Parties Make a Difference?* Macmillan Press, London.

Sanches, E., Santana-Pereira, J. & Razzuoli, I. (2018) 'In welfare we trust? Political trust in Portugal and Spain, 2008-2014', in *Changing Societies: Legacies and Challenges – Citizenship in Crisis*, eds M. Costa Lobo, F. Carreira da Silva & J. P. Zúquete, ICS, Lisbon, pp. 269–294.

Santana-Pereira, J. (2016) 'A esquerda radical no período pós-2009: nada de (muito) novo em Portugal?', *Oficina do Historiador*, vol. 9, no. 1, pp. 58–77.

Santana-Pereira, J. & Cancela, J. (2020). 'Demand without supply? Populist attitudes and voting behaviour in post-bailout Portugal', *South European Society and Politics*, vol. 25, no. 2, pp. 207–230.

Silveira, P., Nina, S. R. & Teixeira, L. H. (2019) *Breve História do Partido Ecologista "Os Verdes" e do Pessoas-Animais-Natureza*, Público and 100Folhas, Lisbon.

Teperoglou, E. & Tsatsanis, E. (2014) 'Dealignment, de-legitimation and the implosion of the two-party system in Greece: the earthquake election of 6 May 2012', *Journal of Elections, Public Opinion and Parties*, vol. 24, no. 2, pp. 222–242.

Tsatsanis, E., Freire, A. & Tsirbas, Y. (2014) 'The impact of the economic crisis on the ideological space in Portugal and Greece: a comparison of elites and voters', *South European Society and Politics*, vol. 19, no. 4, pp. 519–540.

Tsatsanis, E. & Teperoglou, E. (2016) 'Realignment under stress: the July 2015 referendum and the September parliamentary election in Greece', *South European Society and Politics*, vol. 21, no. 4, pp. 427–450.

Tsirbas, Y. (2016) 'The January 2015 parliamentary election in Greece: government change, partial punishment and hesitant stabilisation', *South European Society and Politics*, vol. 21, no. 4, pp. 407–426.

Verney, S. & Bosco, A. (2013) 'Living parallel lives: Italy and Greece in an age of austerity', *South European Society and Politics*, vol. 18, no. 4, pp. 397–426.

Vidal, G. (2018) 'Challenging business as usual? The rise of new parties in Spain in times of crisis', *West European Politics*, vol. 41, no. 2, pp. 261–286.

World Health Organisation (2020) 'WHO Director-General's opening remarks at the media briefing on covid-19-11 March 2020', available online at: https://www.who.int/dg/speeches/detail/who-director-general-s-opening-remarks-at-the-media-briefing-on-covid-19—11-march-2020

How to Combine Public Spending with Fiscal Rigour? 'Austerity by Stealth' in Post-Bailout Portugal (2015–2019)

Catherine Moury(ID), Elisabetta De Giorgi(ID) and Pedro Pita Barros(ID)

ABSTRACT

In this article, we argue that the Costa I Socialist government (2015–2019) managed to combine responsiveness to voters with responsibility towards domestic and international actors by pursuing some kind of 'austerity by stealth', which we define as less visible fiscal contraction that is not displayed by the government in its public discourse. The radical left parties implicitly agreed with this strategy in exchange for the adoption of a long list of visible anti-austerity policies. This allowed the Costa I government to fulfil its electoral pledges and maintain the support of the radical left on the one hand, whilst also reducing the country's deficit and consequently the costs of interest-debt repayments.

The legislative election of October 2015, one year after Portugal had exited the bailout programme, saw the electorate shift to the left. The election was formally won by the incumbent centre right coalition, while the Portuguese Socialist Party (*Partido Socialista* – PS) obtained a positive yet disappointing score (of + 12 seats) and the forces of the radical left – which had previously strongly opposed the austerity measures both in parliament and on the streets – were rewarded by voters. But neither the rightist coalition nor the PS obtained an absolute majority of seats. After lengthy negotiations and the defeat in parliament of a new tentative centre right government, the PS led by António Costa succeeded in forming the first minority government formally supported by the three Portuguese radical left parties: the Left Bloc (*Bloco de Esquerda* – BE), the Portuguese Communist Party (*Partido Comunista Português* – PCP) and the Greens (*Partido Ecologista* – *Os Verdes* – PEV).

Both commentators and rating agencies were concerned that the new Costa government – initially known by the derogatory name of *Geringonça*[1] (contraption) – would not be able to maintain budget discipline (Financial Times 2015). Moreover, few observers would have predicted at the time that the government would reach the end of the legislature (Barros 2019). However, Costa not only stayed in power for the four full years, but during this legislative term (2015–2019) he also managed successfully to conjugate two things thought to be totally incompatible: anti-austerity rhetoric (and policies) and pro-EU stances. Indeed, the government managed to reverse several public spending cuts, halve the unemployment rate, bring the budget deficit to its lowest level in 45 years (Wise 2019) and regain credibility in the markets and at EU level. What is more, the government maintained the external support of the three radical left parties throughout the whole legislature despite their mild euroscepticism and programmatic distance from the PS (Lisi 2016; De Giorgi & Cancela 2019). Finally, in October 2019, the incumbent PS was also able to (re)gain the confidence of the Portuguese voters and was the major winner of the legislative election with 20 more seats in parliament than in 2015.

This success could be interpreted as resulting from the Portuguese government's capacity to respond to 'several principals' (Laffan 2014) as well as to one co-agent. Indeed, given the increasing European and global constraints, parties in government have become 'agents with two principals', that is, delegates of two different subjects: the voters and the European and financial institutions, which sometimes bear conflicting interests (Bardi, Bartolini & Trechsel 2014; Laffan 2014). As the Socialist Party simultaneously met the country's European commitments and fulfilled its electoral pledges to revert many austerity policies (Moury, Cardoso & Gago 2019), it seems to have adequately responded to both its principals. Additionally, it did so by ensuring the support of the radical left – i.e. its 'co-agent' – which was vital for the executive's survival until 2019.[2]

According to some observers (Les échos 2017; New York Times 2018; Financial Times 2019), Costa's triple success was made possible thanks to the boost to demand and production and the fall in unemployment associated with the reversals of the austerity policies. In this article, we argue that this narrative is not entirely accurate and present a three-fold argument. First, we argue that deficit reduction and spending increase within budgetary limits were made possible because the government continued austerity, albeit more discreetly (what we call 'austerity by stealth'). These measures enabled the Portuguese government to reduce the country's deficit in line with the European Monetary Union (EMU) ceilings and, by the same token, to gain credibility with investors. Such an outcome further decreased the cost of interest-debt repayments – which were already lower thanks to the European Central Bank (ECB)[3] – and also gave enough fiscal space to relax the austerity by stealth in the second part of the legislature. Finally, we contend that these measures were accepted by the radical left parties in exchange for the approval of important and visible austerity policy reversals which, following Branco and al., we define as policy changes aimed at neutralising or limiting (temporarily or permanently) the aim of a specific policy (2019, p. 207). We apply the concept of policy reversal to measures enacted in Portugal in the period 2011–2014.

To support our arguments, we rely on a combination of different methods: a number of in-depth interviews with PS government members and radical left MPs, an analysis of the data related to the government spending in its four years in office; and an in-depth examination of the status of the health sector. The paper is thus divided into four sections: the first establishes the theoretical basis of our argument; the second sets the scenes and focuses on the different strategies implemented by the government to achieve its twofold objective – reverting austerity and respecting EU constraints – without upsetting either of its political partners or the markets. The third section analyses the evolution in the government's revenue and spending – with a subsection on the specific case of the National Health System (NHS). A fourth and final section concludes.

Theoretical framework: government's instruments to square the circle

Austerity by stealth

After a period of austerity, parties that campaigned for change find themselves in a tricky situation if they are elected. They have two somehow contradictory interests. On the one hand, they need to satisfy their voters by implementing such a platform. On the other, they have strong incentives to appear credible to investors and respect their international commitments (Moury & Afonso 2019); achieving such goals allows more influence to be gained internationally and/or money to be saved on high interest rates and, in the eurozone, pecuniary sanctions to be avoided. In Peter Mair's eloquent words, governing parties need to be both 'responsive and responsible' (Mair 2009).

Whereas Peter Mair claimed that these were increasingly incompatible goals, we argue that governing parties have a strategy available to them that is both responsive and responsible. This strategy consists of *visibly reverting some austerity measures (and claiming credit for this), while at the same time keeping or even extending less visible cuts and taxes (but not displaying it in public discourse)*. We call this strategy 'austerity by stealth'.

This argument locates itself in a solid body of research that contends governments have incentives to claim credit for popular policies while concealing the implications of less popular choices from voters. For example, welfare state scholars have long shown that programmes susceptible to non-transparent reforms are more likely to be cut than other programmes (Pierson 1996; Lindbom 2007). In a similar vein, Mesa-Lago & Muller (2002) show that policymakers in several Latin American countries concealed the harmful changes associated with pension reforms, drawing public attention to the more visible benefits (see also Carolo 2014 for pensions reforms in Portugal). Exworthy, Macfarlane and Willmott (2009) also demonstrate how the British government obfuscated the reforms of the National Health System.

This strategy has also been studied by economists, in the fiscal sphere. For example, scholars have observed a governmental strategy of 'fiscal illusion' or 'fiscal obfuscation', which means hiding how much citizens pay for the state (for a review see Dollery & Worthington 1996). The main finding of these studies is that a complex tax system helps the government increase public expenditure without taxpayers being fully aware of what is happening (Dell'Anno & Mourao 2011; Sanandaji & Wallace 2010).

A third strand of the literature of relevance to our argument concerns public investments, a category of spending that is often less visible than others in the short term. Statistical analyses show that when fiscal consolidation is required, investment goes down more than other spending categories (see amongst others Breunig & Busemeyer 2012). This is not only true for countries that must respect EMU ceilings, but also for those outside the eurozone (see for example Stancík & Valila 2012). The reason invoked to justify such findings is that public investments are less visible than other expenditure, and hence easier to cut back or postpone (Oxley & Martin 1991, p. 161). Another explanation is that, for some investments, it is companies and not voters that are most affected by the cuts in the short term and parties are more sensitive to the latter when an issue is salient. Studies by Kraft (2017) and Jacques (2019) tested this argument by distinguishing between types of investment, arguing that investments with visible short-term benefits for citizens are more resilient than others. Using different methods, both scholars demonstrate that fiscal pressure makes incumbents cut back on the infrastructure and innovation that most affect companies and universities, rather than on spending related to human capital.

Finally, scholars concerned with the consequences of a bailout for public policy also present interesting findings for our argument. The idea is that spending reversals have costs (lack of budgetary revenues, damaged credibility or EU sanctions) and governments are more likely to reverse policies when this brings an electoral payoff (Moury & Afonso 2019). In this line, Rickard and Caraway (2019) demonstrate that public sector wage cuts made under IMF conditionality do not persist in the longer term because governments are keen to appease powerful domestic constituents. Moury, Cardoso and Gago (2019) show that two-thirds of the spending cuts introduced in Spain and Portugal during the crisis have been reversed, and these reversals were mainly to policies with concentrated benefits and diffuse costs. Finally, Afonso and Bulfone (2019) show how political parties' proposals for reversals are linked to the interests of their core constituencies. All these studies converge in finding that when governments are forced to make budgetary choices, they will maintain (or increase) visible spending and make cuts in less visible areas.

The positive loop

Practising 'austerity by stealth' is not without risk for incumbents, however. First, the opposition and interest groups, who are more informed than ordinary voters, can benefit from alerting citizens about the hidden cuts, especially if they had not been involved in introducing the policy (Elmelund-Præstekær, Klitgaard & Schumacher 2015). Another problem is that under-investment or cuts in less costly areas cannot be kept invisible forever. Firstly, users may notice the degradation of the infrastructure (hospital buildings, classrooms, public transport, etc.) or the deteriorating access to/quality of public services. Also, under-investment reduces growth: for example, Abiad, Furceri and Topalova (2015) used a sample of 17 OECD economies since 1985 to show that a lack of investment decreases growth, restricts private investment and reduces employment.[4] Additionally, a lack of investment in public services is visible to the specific constituencies that would have benefited from it (Kraft 2017; Jacques 2019).

The last point of our argument, however, brings a more positive outlook. We argue that 'austerity by stealth' ultimately creates a positive loop that enables a partial relaxation of this austerity. This is because some degree of hidden austerity allows for a reduction in the deficit that helps boost credibility among investors (and, in the eurozone, avoid EU sanctions). Governments issue bonds to borrow money for short-term or long-term loans at varying rates of interest (yields). The more investors fear the government will default on its debt repayment, the lower the demand for these bonds will be and the higher the yields. Given the substantial size of most government debt burdens, a decrease in bond prices entails significant real savings for the government, which might then be used to (partially) compensate for those hidden austerity measures.

Many other factors impact investors' trust in sovereign bonds, such as elections and the ideology of the incumbents (Ferrara & Stalter 2018), fiscal policies (Tavares 2004), government budgetary plans (McMenamin, Breen & Muñoz-Portillo 2015), concentration of power within the political system (McMenamin & Breen 2013), appointment of technocrats (Alexiadou, Gunaydin & Spaniel 2018), membership of international organisations (Gray 2013), delegation to supranational actors (McMenamin & Breen 2013), and EU declarations and ECB actions (Demertzis & Wolff 2016).

This literature generally converges in affirming that (variation in) fiscal deficits,[5] debt and inflation (in economics, the 'fundamentals') are the most important determinants of the government bond yields. To put it simply, the lower the deficit, debt and inflation, the greater the demand for sovereign bonds will be and the lower the yields (see, amongst others, McMenamin & Breen 2013). In the first years of the EMU, investors in the EMU did not scrutinise these fundamentals closely, and yields were low for all countries. However, when the manipulation of Greece's public account data in 2009 was revealed, investors lost confidence in the ability of some countries to repay their debts, and variation in deficit and debt has since become an important determinant of the yields of sovereign bonds yet again (Wollmershäuser & Klepsch 2011; Poghosyan 2014).

Based on these findings, we thus argue that the reduction in the deficit obtained thanks to austerity by stealth allows a given country to regain credibility vis-a-vis investors and that the associated decrease in borrowing costs might allow a (partial) relaxation of this type of austerity nearer to the elections. This partial improvement increases (slightly) the satisfaction of the users of public services and of organised interests; and makes it more difficult for opposition parties to criticise the government for continued austerity measures.

The Portuguese case: 'contracted austerity by stealth'

Applying our argument to the Portuguese case, we claim that the Costa I government managed to 'square the circle' of reverting many spending cuts while continuing to reduce the deficit (Fernandes, Magalhães & Santana-Pereira 2018, p. 512) not simply due to the (rather timid) economic recovery (Blanchard & Portugal 2017) but also because it continued to pursue some kind of austerity, albeit less visibly than before.

One further issue arises from this argument, however: if the Portuguese government pursued austerity by stealth, how did it manage to maintain the support of the radical left parties? To varying degrees, these parties did not endorse European rules and, as they were not formally in government, felt to some extent free of responsibility. We argue that the mechanism enacted to allow the PS to pursue austerity by stealth was that of the so-called 'contract parliamentarism' or contract minority government (Aylott & Bergman 2004; for Portugal see De Giorgi & Santana-Pereira 2016; Fernandes, Magalhães & Santana-Pereira 2018; De Giorgi & Cancela 2019).

In contract parliamentarism, minority governments 'have relationships with their "support" parties that are so institutionalised that they come close to being majority governments' (Bale & Bergman 2006, p. 422). The party in government signs 'an explicit written contract' with one or more party groups that remain outside the cabinet but give external support to the executive. The agreement usually has the following basic characteristics: it commits the partners 'beyond a specific deal or a temporary commitment' and is 'available to the public' (Bale & Bergman 2006, p. 424). Not only should these characteristics help the party in government maintain the support of the smaller parties through the exchange of policy gains, but they should also enable the supporting parties to influence the content of government policies. As the agreements are public, the pledges within them and their relative fulfilment can be tested by both the electorate and the parties themselves.

In addition to compromises reached in specific areas, as seen in Sweden in 1998 and 2002, in New Zealand in 2005 (Bale & Bergman 2006, p. 436), and in many coalition countries (Timmermans 2006; Moury 2013), a written agreement also implies that partners 'agree to disagree'. This means that the partners do not commit to cooperate on issues that are not included in the pacts, but they accept their partners' stances on these issues. In other words, written agreements involve a pact of non-aggression on those other issues.

We thus argue that the Costa I government managed to pursue austerity by stealth because it made a commitment to pass a series of visible anti-austerity policies through written contracts with the radical left and, in exchange, the latter implicitly accepted the EU constraints. In other words, our third argument is that 'austerity by stealth' was in some way part of a contract with the radical left, which, in exchange for a rapid reversal of visible austerity policies, made an implicit deal to respect Portugal's European commitments, such as keeping the general/structural deficit below 3 per cent/0.5 per cent of Gross Domestic Product (GDP).[6] Hence, the radical left parties tacitly accepted that the costs of the reversals would, if necessary, be covered by less visible spending cuts and/or tax increases.

Setting the scene

The Portuguese bailout and its immediate aftermath (2008-2014)

In May 2011, the Portuguese authorities signed two MoUs (one with the European Union and another with the International Monetary Fund), in which they committed to a series of reforms in exchange for a €78 billion bailout. The MoUs foresaw actions on deficit reduction (notably by cutting spending in education, pensions and health; lowering transfers to regional and local authorities; and reducing public sector employment); competitiveness (reduction of severance payments, labour reforms and liberalisation of the public sector); deleveraging of banks and reforms to the judicial system. This programme was largely implemented by the right-wing coalition of PSD (*Partido Social Democrata* – Social Democratic Party) and CDS-PP (Centro Democrático Social-Partido Popular – Social Democratic Centre Popular Party) coalition, elected a few weeks after the signature of the MoUs (Moury et al. 2020), under the supervision of the troika (European Commission, IMF and the ECB).

During the bailout, GDP growth plummeted and government deficits soared (Guillén & Pavolini 2015). Unemployment rose dramatically and the provision of public services was considerably weakened (Petmesidou & Glatzer 2015). This deterioration had dramatic consequences in a country with a 'dualist' welfare state – that is, with peaks of generosity for some groups and residual protection for others (Ferrara & Sattler 2018). To some extent, the reforms that the troika pushed for moderated the privileges of some and therefore reduced inequality (Perez & Matsaganis 2018). However, those who were already very vulnerable were further impoverished. For example, social protection was considerably weakened. Others have also noted that the cuts in public services led to a serious reduction in access, equity and the quality of health services (Petmesidou & Glatzer 2015).

In May 2014, Portugal exited the programme but remained under an excessive deficit procedure until June 2017; this procedure entails closer scrutiny of the country's actions and failure to meet the goals and deadlines set by the Council can lead to sanctions. Although Portugal's bond yields remained high, they were lowered following the programme of quantitative easing which the ECB Governing Council introduced a few months later, in January 2015 (Hodson 2015). When elections were held in October 2015, the ten-year yield had exceeded 3 per cent. By the end of the year, growth was positive for the first time since the bailout, public debt was over 130 per cent and the public deficit was slightly higher than 3 per cent (see Figure 1).

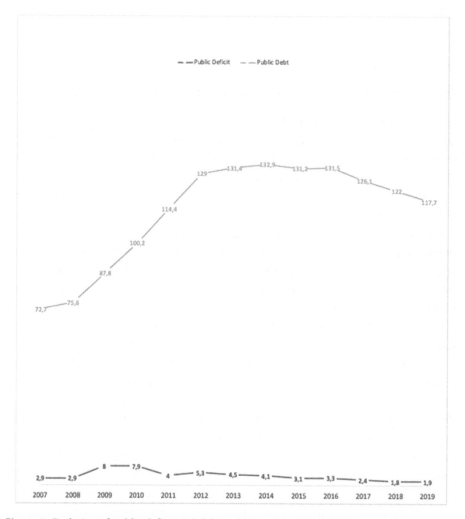

Figure 1. Evolution of public deficit and debt in Portugal, 2007–2019 (as % of GDP).
Source: Budget Office/Ministry of Finance; Bank of Portugal; Statistics Portugal. All collected by Pordata.pt.

The (Implicitly) contracted EU commitments and austerity by stealth

In the 2015 election, the centre right parties together obtained more seats than the PS and could therefore defeat it in any vote in which the three radical left parties abstained or voted against. After a first period of negotiations, the President of the Republic nominated the incumbent PSD leader Pedro Passos Coelho as *formateur*, despite the evident lack of a parliamentary majority. The new government fell after less than 2 weeks following a motion of censure supported by all the left-wing parties (De Giorgi & Santana-Pereira 2016). The left parties' desire to avoid a second right-wing government then paved the way for a minority government led by the Socialist António Costa and supported, for the first time, by the radical left (Lisi 2016).

It should be noted that the three radical left parties clearly chose not to share office with the PS, despite the socialists reiterating the invitation to do so. The decision was probably due to the parties trying to limit potential criticisms from their respective electorate, and they were able to maintain this position as they were numerically essential for the formation and survival of a socialist government. Such an alliance was also facilitated by the PS' clear stance against austerity during the campaign. For instance, in a letter published in the newspaper *Jornal de Negócios* in August 2015, António Costa had affirmed that the austerity adopted by the incumbent government in the previous years had not been fruitful and a reversal of the trend was necessary:

> Despite brutal austerity and enormous impoverishment, we have not grown more, nor do we owe less. (...) We are no longer at the stage of asking whether it is possible to break with austerity, but at a time to say that the austerity page needs to be turned (Jornal de Negócios 2015[7]).

The PS leader's aversion to austerity was evident in public discourse and helped in the negotiation phase after the election, in which the PS discussed and finally signed three bilateral (but similar) agreements with the Left Bloc, the Communist Party and the Greens. The agreements were interpreted as fulfilling the office and policy goals of the socialists and the radical left, respectively (Lisi 2016; De Giorgi & Cancela 2019).

Taken together, the agreements contained over a hundred specific commitments to revert policies to the pre-crisis status quo as well as to adopt various new policies (De Giorgi & Cancela 2019; Fernandes, Magalhães & Santana-Pereira 2018). It is true to say that many of these policies were temporary and supposed to be reverted as soon as the situation improved (the 'extraordinary' income and pensions taxes and civil servants' pay cuts). In some cases, this was even a legal obligation after a Constitutional Court ruling and, here, the Socialist and radical left parties only disagreed on the speed of the reversals and were able to find a compromise. Finally, there was a list of issues on which all the parties agreed that action was necessary but did not share a common position on the specific type of action.[8]

According to our interviewees from the PS and the radical left, negotiations with the BE and the PCP and PEV occurred in two different ways. The leader of the BE, Catarina Martins, had specified during a debate in the electoral campaign that the PS should abandon three specific pledges of its electoral manifesto if they were to enter into negotiations, namely on pensions, the labour code and funding of social security (Botelho 2019). As the PS accepted this condition, negotiations started even before the election and an understanding was reached. With the PCP and PEV, negotiations only started after the elections and were more about listing points of agreement (Interview 3). As a negotiator from the PS explains:

> With the PCP, it was as if we were mentally building a column where we converged, and a column where we diverged, and then we would decide the degree of convergence depending on the weight of each column (Interview 3).

Although the PS certainly insisted during the negotiations on the need to respect the European rules on the deficit and debt reduction (Interview 3), no joint position on the EU, euro and debt renegotiation was included in any of the agreements (PS & BE 2015; PS & PCP 2015; PS & PEV 2015). According to our interviewees, this was a very delicate topic that was dealt with very cautiously. On the PS side, negotiations were opened by saying they intended to comply with the European rules and all the recovery measures had to be achievable within that limit (Interview 1, 3, 5). On the other hand, the radical left acknowledged the PS commitment to European rules but refused to be bound by them. As an interviewee from the BE told us, for example: 'The European commitments of the Socialist Party were well-known to us, but the agreements did not turn the PS commitments into the Left Bloc's commitments' (Interview 5). Nevertheless, several references are made to the need to respect the European rules in the governmental programme that was presented and discussed in parliament (Governo Constitucional 2015).

The first state budget was the most difficult to approve (Interview 1). Its first draft was presented in February 2016 and included several reversals of the policies approved by the previous centre right government. For instance, the income tax surcharge (for higher incomes) was abrogated and additional tax brackets were reintroduced, while pre-bailout working hours, salaries and bonuses in the public sector were reinstated – although the increased contribution to a special health insurance was maintained.[9] As a result, the European Commission (EC) warned that the deficit would be excessive, and that Portugal's level of competitiveness was in danger. The news was received by the government with concern, not only because Portugal was still subject to an excessive deficit procedure but also because ministers saw a causal relationship between the EC budget assessment and that of investors (Moury et al. 2020). As a former junior minister (*secretário de estado*) explained to us:

> One of the reasons why we want[ed] deficit targets to be met and accepted by the EC is that we want[ed] to reassure the financial markets. A country like Portugal gains a lot from having the EC saying "yes sir, this is an acceptable pace of deficit reduction". So, let's say that the concern about the way markets react to our goals is an integral part of our goals (Interview 2).

According to our informants, although the radical left parties were sceptical about the role investors ought to play in politics, the argument employed in negotiations with them was that it was important to appear credible to investors (Interview 2). The solution for the 2016 budget found by the negotiators, and accepted by the radical left, was to cover the increase in expenditure by raising revenues through higher taxes on alcohol, tobacco, vehicles and banking contributions (Moury et al. 2020). As a result, the state budget was approved by the PS, BE, PCP and PEV for the first time in Portuguese history.

In the successive budgets, reversals continued and were deepened or completed, distributing benefits to crucial constituencies of all the parties involved (Fernandes, Magalhães & Santana-Pereira 2018; Moury, Cardoso & Gago 2019). Among others, the government and its partners further increased the lowest level of pensions and social allowances and re-established the pre-bailout conditions for these benefits and the possibility of progressions in the civil service. By the end of 2016, Portugal's economic context was improving as growth started to pick up and yields to decline. Thanks to this, the deficit went down and Portugal exited the excessive deficit procedure in June 2017, moving from the corrective to the preventive arm of the Stability and Growth Pact (Moury, Cardoso & Gago 2019).

Our interviewees pointed out that reaching the two per cent deficit for 2016, an even lower point than forecast and the lowest in 40 years, was fundamental to prove their capability and regain credibility with the EC and the investors:

> There is no doubt that there is a sort of stigma in having an adjustment programme to accomplish. But it is not insurmountable. It is something that can be overcome with credibility and realistic actions. The idea is not to promise a lot and then fall short. It is better to promise what you think you can achieve and then do better (Interview 4).

In line with our second argument, interviewees reported that regaining the confidence of investors (together with the quantitative easing of the ECB), and the related gradual reduction in yields, permitted important budgetary savings. As explained in detail by one of our interviewees:

> We were criticised by the Left Bloc and the PCP because we had reached the 1.4 [deficit] that was already very low and did not invest this money in public utilities, like the NHS.

> But the truth is that achieving that allowed us to put public debt at very low interest
> rates, and this was good because it allowed us to save money on interest (Interview 3).

Just as in the campaign, this fiscal consolidation was not publicly acknowledged. On the contrary. For instance, in an interview with the Spanish newspaper El País in late 2017, the Minister of Economy at the time, Manuel Caldeira Cabral, stated that the government had simultaneously 'ended austerity' in Portugal and regained the investors' confidence. 'We freed the economy from the austerity strings. We ended austerity and adopted a moderate and responsible policy, returned income to workers and pensioners and ensured that citizens would no longer have cuts' (El Pais 2017).[10] Similarly, during the PS Congress in May 2018 when António Costa was re-elected Secretary General, he stated yet again that his government 'proved it is possible to turn the austerity page without leaving the euro'.[11]

Finally, it must be noted that researchers calculated that about 90 per cent of the concrete commitments in the PS-radical left agreements were implemented by the end of 2018 (De Giorgi & Cancela 2019). Most of the pledges that were not fulfilled at the end of the term involved large investments in different areas – for example, improving users' access to the National Health Service and the modernisation of the train services (De Giorgi & Cancela 2019) – a finding that tentatively supports our first argument.

To conclude, it was essential for the government to sign a contract with its supporting parties in order to reach its objectives, i.e. to conjugate two things that were thought to be incompatible: anti-austerity policies (albeit with the limitations that we have mentioned), and pro-EU stances. Respect for the EU rules was not in the contract, but all the left parties gave it their implicit agreement. Austerity by stealth allowed the government to ensure credibility among the EU institutions, the markets and the investors and led to a reduction in yields and an increase in the government's room for improvement in the successive budgets, generating the positive loop that took the country out of the crisis and touching zero deficit in 2019. Less visible tax increases or budgetary cuts were tolerated by the radical left in view of the accomplishment of other policy gains, which also proved to be positive for the PS in the next election campaign.

A quantitative analysis of government spending and revenue

In this section, we show how the choices above were translated into macro-economic outcomes. We show that although the government reverted several austerity policies, there was no inversion of the fiscal contraction in effect since the crisis. Additionally, we look at the consequences of this trend in terms of public services offered to citizens in the health sector.

Public debt

In Figure 1, we show the results of those trends in terms of public debt and deficit (as a percentage of GDP). We can see that the public deficit was in constant decline from 2011 (the first year of the bailout), reaching 1.9 per cent in 2019. Public debt stabilised after 2013 but decreased after 2017. This shows that the Costa I government was indeed responsible for its EU commitments. The ratio of public debt to GDP fell in the last years of the Costa I government as a result of GDP growth being larger than nominal debt increases. The decline in the public debt interest rate contributed significantly to this evolution, due to both international market conditions and the steady improvement in the Portuguese Government's reputation.

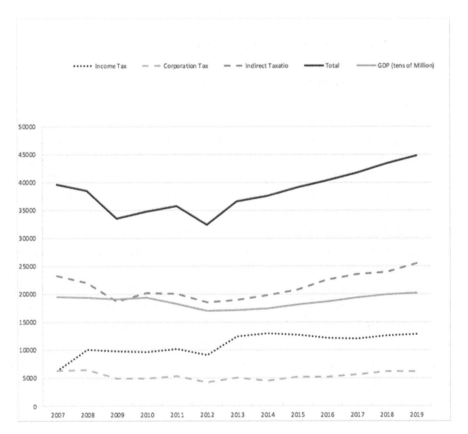

Figure 2. Government revenue in Portugal (2007–2019) by category (in millions of euros at constant price).

Source: Authors' own elaboration from DGO/MF ('report on General State Account') and INE ('Annual Accounts'), collected by Pordata.pt and consulted on 27 August 2020.
Note: References prices are those of 2016. GDP is presented in tens of millions.

Revenues

Fiscal consolidation can be achieved by an increase in taxes and/or a decrease in spending. Starting with the former, Figure 2 depicts the amount of direct and indirect revenues of the Portuguese government from 2007 to 2019, together with the total revenues and the evolution of GDP. We present absolute values at constant prices (the reference year is 2016). Although these figures are traditionally presented as a percentage of GDP, we prefer to present absolute numbers given the marked variation in growth rate during the period under study. However, we add the total GDP to the graph to show how this variation compares with growth in revenues. Both the numerator and the denominator in the usual ratio changed during this period.

In this figure, we can see that GDP started to grow from 2014 onwards, following seven years of low – or even negative (during the bailout years) – growth. Looking at total state revenues, we see that after decreasing from 2008 to 2012 they rose gradually until the end of 2019 (to higher than the pre-crisis level). In other words, there is no indication of a relaxation of fiscal consolidation on the revenue side during the first mandate of the PS, despite an increase in GDP.

A closer examination of the sub-categories of revenues shows an even more interesting picture. On the one hand, we observe that the revenues from income tax, which had risen remarkably in 2013, tended to decrease slightly after the elections (despite the growth in employment and as a result of an increase in the number of tax brackets, which made taxation lower and more progressive as described above). Corporate tax revenues remained stable after the bailout due to the contrasting effect of both a change in the tax rate (which was lowered from 25 per cent to 23 per cent in 2014 and to 21 per cent in 2015) and the increase in economic growth.

On the other hand, revenues from indirect taxes grew more than GDP during the Costa I government as taxes on petrol, sugary drinks, and net worth were raised, while VAT rates that had gone up during the crisis were maintained (except for the taxation on restaurants). Taken together, these results provide support for our austerity by stealth argument: in addition to the relative weight of taxation not going down during the Socialist government, there was a clear shift from visible (income) to less visible (indirect) taxation.

Expenditure

In Figure 3, we turn to Government expenditure. We present the evolution of the most important categories of government spending (in constant prices) since 2007. To understand this evolution, it must be noted that there was no privatisation of public utilities in these sectors contrary to what happened to public spending in transportation, energy and communication, for example.

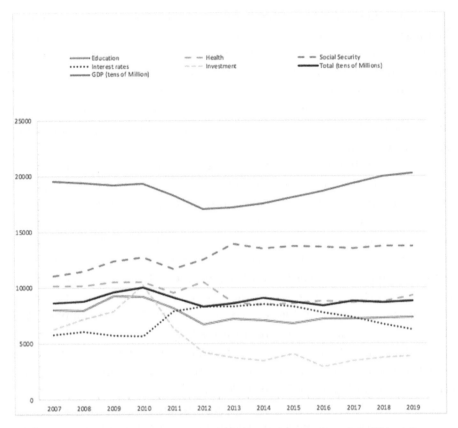

Figure 3. Government spending in Portugal (2007–2019) by category (in millions of euros at constant price).

Source: Authors' own elaboration from DGO/MF ('report on General State Account') and INE ('Annual Accounts'), collected by Pordata.pt and consulted on 27 August 2020.
Note: References prices are those of 2016. GDP is presented in Tens of Millions.

In the figure, we observe an abrupt increase in expenditure on interest rate payments in 2010–12. After the President of the European Central Bank, Mario Draghi, declared his intention to buy national bonds on the secondary market in 2012, the spending on interest rates stabilised for three years. The expenditure on interest rates then went down slightly after 2015 when the BCE started its quantitative easing programme, but this decline became more marked after 2016 when the government deficit started to decrease. Even though it is very difficult to disentangle the effects of the BCE interventions and reduction in government deficit, the sharper decrease in interest payments in 2017, 2018 and 2019 supports our second argument, namely, that the reduction in Portugal's deficit reassured investors and allowed for considerable savings in interest payments. In the case of social security, there had been a counter-cyclical increase during the 2010–12 period (as a result of unemployment), and again a stable pattern from 2013.

The same figure also shows the sharp decrease in total state expenditure and the total spending on education, investment and health in 2010–2012/3, before becoming more or less stable. In other words, we do not observe any increase in spending in absolute terms (or welfare state expansion) relative to post-bailout. If we look at the evolution of GDP, we then can see that the evolution of spending has not accompanied the increase in GDP that started in 2014. In other words, public expenditure as a percentage of GDP declined during the Costa I government.

The most striking feature is the decrease in spending on investment in real terms (and thus the even greater decline as a percentage of GDP since 2014): there had been a dramatic fall in the period 2010 to 2012, which subsequently continued. This is a worrying trend as economists generally agree that public investment tends to foster long term growth, to such an extent that it 'pays for itself' and more (see for example Abiad, Furceri & Topalova 2015). This trend has been observed for both 'hard' (infrastructure) and 'soft' (education, R&D, family support, and active labour market policy) public investment (Streeck & Mertens 2011) in other countries (Hickey, Lozej & Smyth 2018; Hauptman 2018). Moreover, this decline cannot be explained by a closing of public-private partnerships, which are long-term contracts between government and a private-sector company to finance, build, and implement projects (Direção-Geral do Tesouro e Finanças 2012).

However, in line with our positive loop hypothesis, we observe a slight increase in absolute spending the year(s) before the election in two sectors: investment and health. The symmetrical (but larger) fall in interest-rate payments therefore allowed for both this increase and the reduction of the deficit that we observed in Figure 1.

To conclude, we find no evidence of the reversal of austerity on either the revenue or expenditure side. On the contrary, we observe an increase in government revenues and a stabilisation of expenditure at the post-bailout level (that implies that the expenditure in percentage of GDP fell). As expected, despite the government's public statements (see below), its strategy has been to shift from more visible to less visible austerity – namely with relatively more indirect taxation and a significant decrease in investment.

Austerity by stealth in the health sector

The absolute figures for spending and expenditure do not tell us the whole story. Indeed, these numbers do not account for the fluctuation in population, wages, prices and costs that occurred during and after the bailout. To address this limitation, we now turn to a more fine-grained analysis of one key sector of the state, the provision of health services. This area was chosen as it represents the state's major area of spending. It is also very important to the Portuguese: in a poll conducted just before the 2019 election, a quarter of the respondents considered health the most important issue facing the country.

Since 2007, there have been dramatic changes in expenses in the health sector. On the one hand, the immediate impact of the bailout was a drop of circa 14.5 per cent in public health care expenditure in 2012 (the lowest point) vis a vis 2010 (the highest point). Several measures were taken to cut nominal public health care expenditure (Barros 2012). After a first set of measures directed towards civil servants, including wage cuts and an increase in working hours, pharmaceutical spending was the next target; the regulated margins of pharmacies in prescription-only drugs were revised down, a new less costly system of international reference pricing for drugs was introduced as well as health technology assessment methodologies for new pharmaceutical products. Finally, a more diverse bundle of measures sought to increase the efficiency (and lower the costs) of health care delivery (including centralised procurement initiatives, imposition of price reductions on service and product providers, better management of human resources, etc.). With the end of the bailout period and the change in government, the first set of measures affecting the wages and working hours of NHS workers was gradually reversed. Also, new pharmaceutical products, introduced mainly in the hospital market, have considerably higher prices than the products in the same therapeutic class that had previously been introduced. There is now less pressure to contain the new prices.

We examine the effects of these changes from four different angles. We first present a statistical analysis of the trends in different categories of expenditure, before making a detailed analysis of the evolution of the hospital debts, the waiting list for various procedures and the citizens' perception of whether their needs are met.

In the statistical analysis of the *trends* in expenditure in different indicators of health services, we distinguish three distinct time periods: before the bailout (2000–2011), during the bailout (2011–2014) and after the bailout (post-2014). We use a simple regression model to compute mean effects:

$$x_i = a_0 + a_1 t \times D_1 + a_2 t \times D_2 + a_3 t$$

where t represents a time trend variable, D_1 takes value 1 during years 2011–2014, value 0 otherwise and D_2 takes value 1 during years 2015–2017 (or later) and value 0 before 2015. a_1 and a_2 coefficients represent the change in a given indicator during the bailout period and afterwards, respectively. Hence, coefficients should be interpreted as deviations from the previous time trend evolution. The small number of years implies that this exercise should be seen primarily as a useful description of the main features of this period.

If neither coefficient is different from zero, there has been no change in trend since the initial period. Negative/positive coefficients imply that austerity/fiscal expansion is at play in a given period. When both coefficients are negative, if a_1

is inferior (more negative)/superior to a_2, it could be said that austerity was attenuated/aggravated (respectively) in the later period.[12]

To put it simply, the analysis is based on the idea of deviations to a trend. The growth of spending in a given category during the troika period (2012–2014) and after (2015–2017) is measured against the trend of growth before the troika (2000–2011). The next table summarises the main results of the regression analysis as described by the equation above.[13] In Table 1, we observe that austerity in the health sector took place during the bailout years, but subsequently continues: if we consider the total public health expenditure,[14] we can see that a_1 and a_2 are negative and statistically significant – which means there was a downward trend in expenditure as compared to the previous period.

Cuts in public expenditure can result from cutting services, costs and prices and shifting payment from the public sector to households. We therefore identify the trends in a range of different expenditures. We look at all the sub-types of expenditure for hospital care and we observe fiscal contraction during the bailout, but also for inpatient and outpatient care in the post-bailout period. We find that neither the bailout nor its termination had a significant impact on the expenditure trend for daycare. Similarly, there was a negative shift in the trend in spending on pharmaceutical goods for both the bailout and post-bailout periods.

We can assess whether households had to cover an increasing part of the bill by looking at the evolution of out-of-pocket payments, i.e. the sum paid by citizens and not reimbursed by the NHS, including the user charges in hospitals, cost-sharing for drugs, etc. To recall, the increase in user charges for some public services was a landmark decision under the international financial assistance programme (although coupled with an increase in exemptions from these charges) and these were later reduced by the new government in early 2016. To account for the effect of these changes, the same statistical analysis is performed using out-of-pocket payments (last row of Table 1). We can see a downward trend in the amount of out-of-pocket payments both during and after the bailout. More precisely, Table 1 shows that while out-of-pocket

Table 1. Main result of the regression analysis of the trends in expenditure for different budget categories.

Dependent variable	(a_1) 2011–2014	(a_2) 2015–2017	Test $a_1 = a_2$ $F(1,14))$	Interpretation
Public health expenditure	−144*	−166*	Does not reject	Austerity by stealth
Public inpatient expenditure	−27*	−28*	Does not reject	Austerity by stealth
Public hospital day care expenditure	2,8	2,7	Does not reject	No austerity impact
Public outpatient expenditure	−46*	−60*	Does not reject	Austerity by stealth
Public expenditure with pharmaceuticals	−43*	−47*	Does not reject	Austerity by stealth
Out-of-pocket payments by households (total)	−48*	−58*	Does not reject	Health system improvement

Source: own computation, based on INE – Health National Accounts.
Note: * means statistically significant at the 5% level; a negative sign for coefficients means a lower growth compared with the trend in 2000–2010.

payments by households during the troika years did not increase, this out-of-pocket expenditure does then increase but the pace of growth is nearly identical to the trend before the troika years.

In Table 1, we can therefore infer that there has been no reversal in austerity, as measured by the evolution in health expenditure. After the bailout, there was still fiscal consolidation in expenditure for care in hospitals (excluding day care) and for pharmaceuticals. Hence, the emerging picture is one of austerity falling upon providers of care within the scope of the NHS, with public hospitals and pharmaceuticals being particularly affected. There is not, however, evidence of the government shifting its public expenditure to households during this period.

Another important indicator of financial constraints faced by public hospitals is the amount of debt they create. This debt creation, and the subsequent immediate growth in arrears, has always represented one of the escape doors from budget limitations in the management of hospitals. Consequently, the total amount of arrears (payments due that exceed delays of 180 days) could be taken as a summary indicator of the insufficiency of hospital funds to meet their medical assistance needs. This indicator is available with monthly periodicity and is presented in Figure 4 (a sudden drop usually suggests that extra funds were made available).

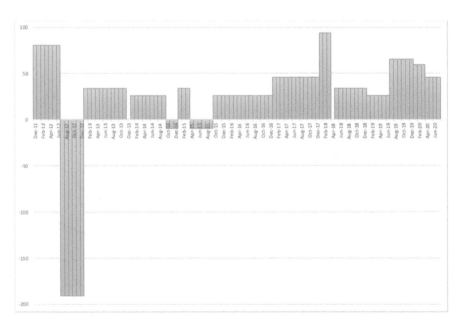

Figure 4. Average monthly growth in arrears in debts of NHS hospitals in Portugal, per trend period.

Source: Authors' own computations, based on the values of monthly arrears by the Portuguese Direction General of Budget.

Note: Arrears are, by definition, the payments of public sector delayed more than 180 days. Equal values over consecutive months means the same average trend value applies.

At the start of the bailout, the existing hidden debts were brought into the accounting system. The drop observed in July 2012 is explained by the extra funds made available to regularise hospital debt. Subsequently, arrears had a monthly absolute growth of *circa* 30.8 million euros. From June 2014 to August 2019, and again excluding the effect of debt regularisation transfers, there was a monthly growth in arrears of 30.7 million euros. If we consider only the Costa I government, the mean absolute growth in arrears was 39.2 million euros per month. Therefore, the end of the international financial assistance programme did not stop the financial pressure on hospitals; quite the contrary. This finding again provides support for the argument that the socialist government pursued austerity by stealth.

Another escape door for hospitals facing contraction is that of delaying the provision of services, with waiting times being used to avoid more health expenditure.[15] Figure 5 reports information on median waiting times for the most important types of surgeries and their recent evolution as an illustration of the general movement. It shows that the austerity years were associated with an

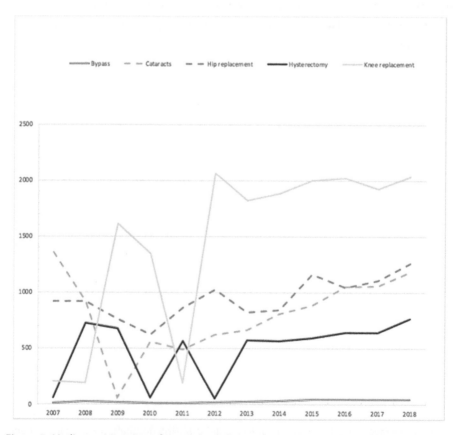

Figure 5. Median waiting times for surgery in Portugal in 2007–2019 (number of days).
Source: Authors' own elaboration from OECD Health Data 2019.

increase in waiting times; however, the effect has not disappeared in more recent years and, in some cases, it is quite the opposite. This information again corroborates the austerity by stealth argument.

A final piece of information about service quality comes from the unmet medical needs indicator from the EU-SILC (European Union Statistics on Income and Living Conditions) survey. Figure 6 shows the percentage of citizens who had an unmet health care need due to costs, distance or waiting lists in the previous year.[16] We can observe an increase in unmet needs during the austerity years (2011–2014), with a reversal afterwards – a similar evolution pattern is found in the EU. Hence, the austerity by stealth situation did not deter the patients' first contact with the NHS (or the health system, more generally), and the containment of public health expenditure occurred therefore through increased waiting times, and with increases in debt and arrears.

What emerges is that the cut in costs in both the bailout and post-bailout periods caused a deterioration in the quality of public services and delayed services (together with a reduction in the profit of the pharmaceutical industry and pharmacies) but it did not leave people unattended on a large scale. Overall, we find important evidence in support of our argument that unrecognised austerity, i.e. austerity by stealth, has been pursued by the Socialist government to square the circle.

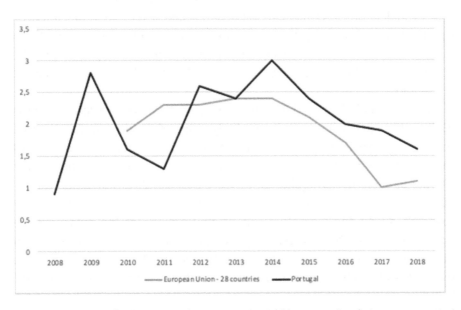

Figure 6. Percentage of citizens reporting an unmet need (due to services being too expensive) in the past year.

Source: Authors' own elaboration from Eurostat data.

Conclusions

In this article, we bring some nuance to the narrative that suggests the Portuguese recovery – and the subsequent reduction of the debt and deficit – was made possible thanks to the ending of austerity, which gave rise to more growth and revenue. We argue and demonstrate that in addition to the more visible reversals of austerity policies, the government also pursued some 'austerity by stealth'.

We show that these measures of austerity by stealth were implicitly accepted by the radical left parties whilst negotiating their agreements with the PS in 2015 and when voting on the annual budgets, in exchange for the adoption of a long list of more visible anti-austerity policies. These measures enabled the Portuguese government to reduce the country's deficit in line with the EMU ceilings and, by the same token, to gain credibility with investors and lower the cost of interest-debt repayments.

We further look at the evolution of government spending and revenues and observe a shift from direct to indirect taxation revenue, and the continuity of low spending on health, education and investment. Given the increase in GDP, this continuity means that the relative weight of that spending had decreased. We also observe that from 2018–19 onwards, the decline in spending on interest rates payments allowed the government to (partially) increase investments and health spending – without reaching the level of the pre-troika years however.

To glean a deeper understanding of what this decrease means, we take a closer look at one specific field: the health sector. There, we find evidence of a prolongation of austerity despite the rise in health workers' wages and the cut in their working hours. However, the burden of this austerity was carried by hospitals and the pharmaceutical stakeholders rather than directly by households.

Finally, it should be noted that this strategy was electorally successful for the PS. Even though citizens were increasingly aware of the deterioration in public services, notably in health and transportation (a central issue in the 2019 campaign), the incumbent PS gained seats and votes in the election. On the left, the BE more or less replicated its (very positive) 2015 outcome, while the CDU – i.e. the PCP and the Greens, which had claimed the credit for visible spending during the legislature but blamed the PS for the cuts – suffered significant losses. This is a puzzling fact that warrants further research, but that may be explained, at least in part, by the fact that voters in a country that had just been bailed out now value the state's capacity to keep its accounts in order.

A comparative analysis would help verify whether our findings can be applied to other countries that were equally hit by the economic crisis. Since the anti-austerity rhetoric was quite common in all South European countries in the post-crisis period, notably among the left or challenger parties, the present study on the relationship between responsiveness and responsibility and the strategy adopted by the governing parties to fulfil both should be replicated in further cases, and notably in those in which anti-austerity parties formed governments. The alarming decrease in public investment observed everywhere but especially in Southern Europe indicates that austerity by stealth is probably a widespread phenomenon.

Notes

1. The term 'Geringonça' appeared for the first time in the Portuguese newspaper *Público* in August 2014 to describe the Socialist Party in the campaign for the primary election that opposed António Costa to António José Seguro. The term was later used by the CDS-PP President, Paulo Portas, in a parliamentary debate to describe the PS minority government supported by the radical left (Barros 2019).
2. Even though this government solution was not re-confirmed after the last election and the Socialist Party now governs as a minority without any explicit parliamentary support.
3. The ECB started buying assets from commercial banks in March 2015 as part of its non-standard monetary policy measures. These asset purchases are also known as quantitative easing or QE.
4. Similar findings were found by Dreger and Reimers (2016) and Fournier (2016), among others.
5. Together with inflation, which is no longer the responsibility of national governments within the EMU.
6. The Fiscal Compact obliges ratifying member states to keep their general budget deficit below 3.0 per cent of the GDP, and their structural deficit below their Medium-Term budgetary Objective (MTO) which can be set to a maximum of 0.5 per cent of GDP for states with a debt-to-GDP ratio exceeding 60 per cent – or a maximum of 1.0 per cent of GDP for states with debt levels within the 60 per cent limit.
7. Translated to English by the authors.
8. For instance, 'defending the social functions of the state and public services, social security, education and health, promoting a serious fight against poverty and social and economic inequalities', as stated in all the three agreements signed, without specifying how to reach such objectives.
9. For a list of reverted policies see Moury, Cardoso and Gago (2019).
10. Translated to English by the authors.
11. English translation from 'Provámos que é possível virar a página da austeridade sem sair do euro', TVI24, 26 May 2019:https://tvi24.iol.pt/videos/politica/provamos-que-e-possivel-virar-a-pagina-da-austeridade-sem-sair-do-euro/5b08a0a30cf2c09c9a16589f
12. The interpretation is as follows: $(a_1-a_2) > 0$ – increase in x during the troika was larger than after the troika; $a_1 = a_2$ it is the same; $a_1 \_ a_2 < 0$ – increase in x during the troika was smaller, impact of troika was larger $= >$ thus $a_1 < a_2 < 0$ (a_1 inferior to a_2) means lower impact during period 2 (after troika) than during period 1 (troika).
13. The number of observations is 18, with 14 degrees of freedom.
14. Including both the National Health Service and the Regional Health Services of Azores and Madeira autonomous regions. The analysis is performed in nominal terms (during this period, inflation was generally low, and evolution of out-of-pocket payments was

      driven by both price and volume effects). A revision in the statistical series of the National Health Accounts was made, and the values for 2016–2017 were reviewed upwards relative to the previous series. We do not have further backward compatibility. The main computations above used the old series.

15. Another option for hospitals is the reduction in investment and maintenance of equipment, but unfortunately no detailed analysis of ageing equipment and maintenance and replacement delays is publicly available. However, this possibility is very plausible if we look at the overall trend in investment.

16. Although this indicator has been criticised for being subjective and not related to actual received care (for a discussion of this measure see Allin & Masseria 2009), it still provides useful information.

Disclosure statement

No potential conflict of interest was reported by the author(s).

ORCID

Catherine Moury ⓘD http://orcid.org/0000-0001-5405-1493
Elisabetta De Giorgi ⓘD http://orcid.org/0000-0002-6553-341X
Pedro Pita Barros ⓘD http://orcid.org/0000-0002-0881-4928

List of interviews

(1) Junior Minister, PS Government, 7 May 2018.
(2) Junior Minister, PS Government, 18 May 2018.

(3) Junior Minister, PS Government, 20 June 2018.
(4) Minister, PS Government, 23 May 2018.
(5) Negotiator, BE, 7 November 2019.

References

Abiad, A. D., Furceri, D. & Topalova, P. (2015). 'The macroeconomic effects of public invest-ment: evidence from advanced economies', *Journal of Macroeconomics*, vol. 50, pp. 224–240.

Afonso, A. & Bulfone, F. (2019). 'Electoral coalitions and policy reversals in Portugal and Italy in the aftermath of the eurozone crisis', *South European Society and Politics*, vol. 24, no. 2, pp. 233–257.

Alexiadou, D., Gunaydin, H. & Spaniel, W. (2018) 'Calming the markets: when technocratic appointments signal credibility', Paper presented at the 8th Annual Conference of the European Political Science Association, 21-23 June, Vienna.

Allin, S. & Masseria, C. (2009) 'Research Note: unmet need as an indicator of access to health care in Europe', The London School of Economics and Political Science: European Commission Directorate-General "Employment, Social Affairs and Equal Opportunities" Unit E1–Social and Demographic Analysis.

Aylott, N. & Bergman, T. (2004) 'Almost in government, but not quite: the Swedish Greens, bargaining constraints and the rise of contract parliamentarism', paper presented at the ECPR Joint Sessions of Workshops, Uppsala, 13-18 April.

Bale, T. & Bergman, T. (2006). 'Captives no longer, but servants still? Contract parliamentarism and the new minority governance in Sweden and New Zealand', *Government and Opposition*, vol. 41, no. 3, pp. 422–449.

Bardi, L., Bartolini, S. & Trechsel, A. H. (2014). 'Responsive and responsible? The role of parties in twenty-first century politics', *West European Politics*, vol. 37, no. 2, pp. 235–252.

Barros, P. P. (2012). 'Health policy reform in tough times: the case of Portugal', *Health Policy*, vol. 106, no. 1, pp. 17–22.

Barros, S. (2019). 'Quando um Governo de Esquerda assusta os media - A formação da "geringonça" nos jornais', *Observatorio (OBS*) Journal*, vol. 13, no. 1, pp. 192–211.

Blanchard, O. & Portugal, P. (2017). 'Boom, slump, sudden stops, recovery, and policy options. Portugal and the Euro', *Portuguese Economic Journal*, vol. 16, no. 3, pp. 149–168.

Botelho, L. (2019) 'Catarina Martins mostrou abertura para viabilizar governo do PS antes das eleições de 2015', *Público*, 23 September.

Branco, R., Cardoso, D., Guillén, A. M., Sacchi, S. & Balbona, D. L. (2019). 'Here to stay? Reversals of structural reforms in Southern Europe as the crisis wanes', *South European Society and Politics*, vol. 24, no. 2, pp. 205–232. doi:10.1080/13608746.2019.1640966.

Breunig, C. & Busemeyer, M. R. (2012). 'Fiscal austerity and the trade-off between public investment and social spending', *Journal of European Public Policy*, vol. 19, no. 6, pp. 921–938.

Carolo, D. (2014), 'Despesa e redistribuição na Segurança Social em Portugal: análise da Reforma de 2007', PhD thesis, Instituto das Ciências Sociais, Lisbon.

De Giorgi, E. & Cancela, J. (2019). 'The Portuguese radical left parties supporting government: from policy-takers to policymakers?', *Government and Opposition*, advanced online publication, pp. 1–20. doi:10.1017/gov.2019.25.

De Giorgi, E. & Santana-Pereira, J. (2016). 'The 2015 Portuguese legislative election: widening the coalitional space and bringing the extreme left in', *South European Society and Politics*, vol. 21, no. 4, pp. 451–468.

Dell'Anno, R. & Mourao, P. (2011). 'Fiscal illusion around the world: an analysis using the structural equation approach', *Public Finance Review*, vol. 40, no. 2, pp. 270–299.

Demertzis, M. & Wolff, G. B. (2016) 'The effectiveness of the European Central Banks's asset purchase programme', *Bruegel Policy Contribution*, 2016/10.

Direção-Geral do Tesouro e Finanças, Ministério das Finanças. (2012) 'Boletim Informativo, Parcerias Público-Privadas e Concessões', http://www.dgtf.pt/ResourcesUser/PPP/Documentos/Relatorios/2012/Relatorio_Anual_PPP_2012.pdf.

Dollery, B. & Worthington, A. (1996). 'The empirical analysis of fiscal illusion', *Journal of Economic Surveys*, vol. 10, no. 3, pp. 261–297.

Dreger, C. & Reimers, H. E. (2016). 'Does public investment stimulate private investment? Evidence for the euro area', *Economic Modelling*, vol. 58, pp. 154–158.

El Pais (2017) 'Caldeira Cabral: "Portugal va tener el mayor crecimiento del siglo"', 3 September.

Elmelund-Præstekær, C., Klitgaard, M. B. & Schumacher, G. (2015). 'What wins public support? Communicating or obfuscating welfare state retrenchment', *European Political Science Review*, vol. 7, no. 3, pp. 427–450. .

Exworthy, M., Macfarlane, F. & Willmott, M. (2009). *NHS Management: 60 Years of Transition*, Nuffield Trust, London.

Fernandes, J. M., Magalhães, P. C. & Santana-Pereira, J. (2018). 'Portugal's leftist government: from sick man to poster boy?', *South European Society and Politics*, vol. 23, no. 4, pp. 503–524.

Ferrara, F. M. & Sattler, T. (2018) 'The political economy of financial markets', *Oxford Research Encyclopedia of Politics*.

Financial Times (2015) 'Portugal divided by austerity', 1 December.

Financial Times (2019) 'Portugal: a European path out of austerity?', 10 May.

Fournier, J. M. (2016) *The Positive Effect of Public Investment on Potential Growth*, OECD Publishing, Paris, no. 1347.

Governo Constitucional (2015) 'Programa do XXI Governo Constitucional 2015-2019', https://www.portugal.gov.pt/ficheiros-geral/programa-do-governo-pdf.aspx

Gray, J. (2013). *The Company States Keep: International Economic Organizations and Investor Perceptions*, Cambridge University Press, Cambridge.

Guillén, A. M. & Pavolini, E. (2015). 'Welfare states under strain in Southern Europe: overview of the special issue', *European Journal of Social Security*, vol. 17, no. 2, pp. 147–157.

Hauptman, M. (2018). 'Importance of public investment for economic growth in the European Union', *Public Sector Economics*, vol. 42, no. 2, pp. 131–137.

Hickey, R., Lozej, M. & Smyth, D. (2018). 'Irish government investment, financing and the public capital stock', *Quarterly Bulletin Articles, Central Bank of Ireland*, pp. 64–76.

Hodson, D. (2015). Eurozone Governance: Deflation, Grexit 2.0 and the second coming of Jean-Claude Juncker, *Journal of Common Market Studies*, vol. 53, no. S1, pp. 144–161. doi:10.1111/jcms.12263.

Jacques, O. (2019) *Austerity and the path of least resistance: how fiscal consolidations crowd out future investments*, paper presented at the Conference of the Society for the Advancement of Socio-Economics, 27-29 June, New York.

Jornal de Negócios (2015) 'Carta de António Costa: virar a página da austeridade, relançar a economia', 27 August.

Kraft, J. (2017) 'The Politics of Investment: how Policy Structure Shapes', PhD thesis, Aarhus University.

Laffan, B. (2014). 'Testing times: the growing primacy of responsibility in the Euro Area', *West European Politics*, vol. 37, no. 2, pp. 270–287.

Les échos (2017) 'Portugal's Economic Miracle Makes A Case Against Austerity', 18 July.

Lindbom, A. (2007). 'Obfuscating retrenchment: swedish welfare policy in the 1990s', *Journal of Public Policy*, vol. 1, no. 1, pp. 129–150.

Lisi, M. (2016). 'U-Turn: the portuguese radical left from marginality to government support', *South European Society and Politics*, vol. 21, no. 4, pp. 541–560.

Mair, P. (2009). 'Representative versus Responsible Government' *MPIfG Working Paper* 09/8. Cologne.

McMenamin, I. & Breen, M. (2013). 'Political institutions, credible commitment, and sovereign debt in advanced economies', *International Studies Quarterly*, vol. 57, no. 4, pp. 842–854.

McMenamin, I., Breen, M. & Muñoz-Portillo, J. (2015). 'Austerity and credibility in the Eurozone', *European Union Politics*, vol. 16, no. 1, pp. 45–66.

Mesa-Lago, C. & Müller, K. (2002). 'The politics of pension reform in Latin America', *Journal of Latin American Studies*, vol. 34, no. 3, pp. 687–715.

Moury, C. (2013). *Coalition Government and Party Mandate*, Routledge, London.

Moury, C., et al. (2020). *Capitalising on Constraint: The Politics of Conditionality in Bailed Out Countries during and after the Eurozone Crisis*, Manchester University Press, Manchester.

Moury, C. & Afonso, A. (2019). 'Beyond conditionality: policy reversals in Southern Europe in the aftermath of the eurozone crisis', *South European Society and Politics*, vol. 24, no. 2, pp. 155–176.

Moury, C., Cardoso, D. & Gago, A. (2019). 'When the lenders leave town: veto players, electoral calculations and vested interests as determinants of policy reversals in Spain and Portugal', *South European Society and Politics*, vol. 24, no. 2, pp. 177–204.

New York Times (2018) 'Portugal dared to cast aside austerity. It's having a major revival', 22 July.

Oxley, H. & Martin, J. P. (1991). 'Controlling government spending and deficits: trends in the 1980s and prospects for the 1990s', *OECD Economic Studies*, vol. 17, pp. 145–189.

Perez, S. A. & Matsaganis, M. (2018). 'The political economy of austerity in Southern Europe', *New Political Economy*, vol. 23, no. 2, pp. 192–207.

Petmesidou, M. & Glatzer, M. (2015). 'The crisis imperative, reform dynamics and rescaling in Greece and Portugal', *European Journal of Social Security*, vol. 17, no. 2, pp. 158–181.

Pierson, P. (1996). 'The new politics of the welfare state', *World Politics*, vol. 48, no. 2, pp. 143–179.

Poghosyan, T. (2014). 'Long-run and short-run determinants of sovereign bond yields in advanced economies', *Economic Systems*, vol. 38, no. 1, pp. 100–114.

PS & BE (2015) 'Posição conjunta do Partido Socialista e do Bloco de Esquerda sobre solução política', http://cdn.impresa.pt/284/9c2/9700333/BE.pdf.

PS & PCP (2015) 'Posição conjunta do PS e do PCP sobre solução política', http://cdn.impresa.pt/14d/378/9700329/PCP.pdf

PS & PEV (2015) 'Posição conjunta do PS e do PEV sobre solução política', http://www.osverdes.pt/media/Parlamento/PosicaoConjuntaPS_PEV.pdf

Rickard, S. J. & Caraway, T. L. (2019). 'International demands for austerity: examining the impact of the IMF on the public sector', *The Review of International Organizations*, vol. 14, no. 1, pp. 35–57.

Sanandaji, T. & Wallace, B. (2010) 'Fiscal illusion and fiscal obfuscation: anempirical study of tax perception in Sweden', IFN Working Paper No. 837, available online at: https://ssrn.com/abstract=1619268

Stančík, J. & Välilä, T. (2012). 'Changes in the fiscal stance and the composition of public spending', *Empirical Economics*, vol. 43, no. 1, pp. 199–217.

Streeck, W. & Mertens, D. (2011) 'Fiscal austerity and public investment: is the possible the enemy of the necessary?', MPIfG Discussion Paper 11/12, Max-Planck-Institut für Gesellschaftsforschung.

Tavares, J. (2004). 'Does right or left matter? Cabinets, credibility and fiscal adjustments', *Journal of Public Economics*, vol. 88, no. 12, pp. 2447–2468. doi:10.1016/j.jpubeco.2003.11.001.

Timmermans, A. (2006). 'Standing apart and sitting together: enforcing coalition agreements in multiparty systems', *European Journal of Political Research*, vol. 45, no. 2, pp. 263–283.

Wise, P. (2019) 'Portugal posts lowest budget deficit in 45 years of democracy', *Financial Times*, 26 March.

Wollmershäuser, T. & Klepsch, C. (2011). 'Yield spreads on EMU government bonds—How the financial crisis has helped investors to rediscover risk', *Intereconomics*, vol. 46, no. 3, pp. 169–176.

Party System Renewal or Business as Usual? Continuity and Change in Post-Bailout Portugal

Marco Lisi ⓘ, Edalina Rodrigues Sanches ⓘ and Jayane dos Santos Maia ⓘ

ABSTRACT
The recent economic crisis has created momentum for party system change in most European democracies. While Portugal has shown more predictable patterns of interparty competition, since the 2015 elections it has experienced incremental changes in the electoral, parliamentary and governing arenas. This study explores several dimensions of the Portuguese party system (including volatility, alternation in government and innovation) from a longitudinal perspective, and provides new explanations for its development. Focusing on the post-bailout period, it argues that abstention and party strategy go a long way to explaining the patterns of continuity and (marginal) change in the Portuguese party system.

Since the onset of the Great Recession, dramatic changes have shaken the status quo in European political systems (Chiaramonte & Emanuele 2017; Hutter & Kriesi 2019). Unlike other countries affected by the eurozone crisis, the case of Portugal has been depicted as one of mild changes, with no major electoral earthquakes or realignments (De Giorgi & Santana-Pereira 2016; Sanches 2021; Jalali 2018, 2019).

Despite the overall stability, two important changes have emerged in the post-bailout period. First, an unprecedented level of cooperation between the parties of the left after the 2015 elections led to the emergence of contract parliamentarism[1] based on a government led by the Socialist Party (PS, *Partido Socialista*) with the support of the Portuguese Communist Party (PCP, *Partido Comunista Português*), the Greens (PEV, *Partido Ecologista 'Os Verdes'*) and the Left Bloc (BE, *Bloco de Esquerda*) (Lisi 2016; Fernandes, Magalhães & Santana-Pereira 2018; De Giorgi & Santana-Pereira 2016; Jalali 2018, 2019). Second, new parties entered the parliament following the 2019 legislative elections, namely the left-libertarian *Livre* (L, Free), the economically libertarian *Iniciativa Liberal* (IL, Liberal Initiative) and the populist radical right *Chega* (CH, Enough).

Given these recent changes, is the Portuguese party system still diverging from the trends that characterise other European party systems? Have the 2019 elections furthered the gradual adaptation of the Portuguese system or have they opened a new phase? What factors can explain the evolution of the Portuguese party system?

This article argues that despite the changes experienced in the post-bailout period, the core components of the Portuguese party system have remained stable: the two major parties, PS and PSD, continue to gather the majority of votes and seats and they are still the leading actors for government formation. In addition, we argue that we need to consider both demand and supply side factors to explain the evolution of the Portuguese party system. We test these arguments by examining the patterns of change and continuity in Portugal over the democratic period, with a focus on the post-bailout period (2015–2019). The empirical analyses draw on aggregate electoral data and qualitative sources (e.g. online newspapers, social media activity) to explore the impact of abstention/turnout and party strategies on the patterns observed.

The Portuguese case is worthy of analysis as it has been considered a deviant case (Seawright & Gerring 2008) that goes against the theoretical expectations of party system change. In comparison to other countries, Portugal has displayed high levels of continuity in the patterns of interparty competition even though it was one of the countries most severely hit by the 2008 crisis. This article builds on this deviance to leverage explanations that combine both demand and supply-side factors. In doing so, it offers contributions beyond the case study literature, thus allowing a better understanding of party system change and continuity.

The study proceeds as follows. It starts by setting out the literature on party system change, and how high abstention and party strategy affect party systems. The methodological section presents the data and procedures of the empirical analysis. We then provide a contextualisation of the Portuguese party system over the democratic period to underpin our argument that there has been a fair degree of stability in the party system in the post-bailout period. The following section examines the context and results of the two most recent Portuguese parliamentary elections held in 2015 and 2019. The main empirical sections analyse the impact of turnout and party strategy on the evolution of the party system. The final section summarises our findings and their implications for further research on party system change in contemporary democracies.

Examining party system change

Party system change is not easy to define but it has become increasingly accepted that change can be measured through different parameters and arenas of competition. Mair (1989, p. 257) states that party system change 'occurs when as a result of ideological, strategic, or electoral shift, there is transformation in the direction of competition or the governing formulae' (Mair 1989, p. 257). Mainwaring (1999) posits that a stable party system involves patterned interactions between established parties, and sees change as a sharp discontinuity in the component parts of the system. What is interesting in both definitions is that they set a threshold for change: it must entail a dramatic shift in the rules of interparty competition, and affect the core – rather than the margin – of the party system.

Various indicators have been used to measure change or stability, including electoral volatility – by far the most used indicator (e.g. Pedersen 1990; Chiaramonte & Emanuele 2017) – party system fragmentation (or size), the degree of institutionalisation/fluidity of party systems (e.g. Mainwaring & Scully 1995; Bértoa 2018) and the number of new parties entering the parliament (e.g. Meguid 2005; Tavits 2006, 2008; Lago and Martinez 2010). This diversity gives rise to a lack of consensus on the arenas that need to be considered to examine the transformation of party systems: while the electoral dimension has been more widely studied, thus far the parliamentary and governmental arenas have been more neglected (Bértoa 2018).

Scholars have also advanced several theories of party system change (or stability). Conventional explanations usually consider the effects of the cleavage structure, political institutions, economic performance and electoral participation and their relative importance (Mair 1997; Broughton & Donovan 1998; Pennings & Lane 1998; Wolinetz 1988). Another stream in the literature has focused on party strategies, suggesting that party system change or stability is not only due to external factors but also to the strategies parties pursue to win support 'within parameters set for instance by cleavage structures, institutions, voting patterns and party organisation' (Sitter 2002, p. 429). It is also assumed that parties 'do not use the same calculus in devising their strategies' (Tromp 1989, p. 83) and that they can miscalculate their potential success. Depending on their status, parties might want to prevent or induce change and this is why the strategies they use matters.

We build on this discussion to advance a new explanatory framework for the analysis of the Portuguese party system, the core components of which continue to display a high degree of stability and continuity – despite recent changes. In a nutshell, our argument combines both demand and supply-side factors. The demand-side explanation suggests that high abstention rates have fostered party system stability. Instead of opting for new alternatives, disenchanted voters exited the electoral market, and this ultimately strengthened the position of governing parties. The supply-side argument stresses the importance of party strategies to the explanation of party system change and stability. While credit claiming allowed the PS to demarcate itself from the radical left and strengthen its position in the party system, new parties took advantage of fresh issues and innovative campaign communication strategies to break through (though with marginal success).

The impact of abstention and party strategies

The demand-side explanation posits that higher levels of abstention engender party system stability. Katz and Mair (1995, 2018) have developed this point as part of their theory on the cartelisation of party politics, according to which the increasing dealignment and gradual exit of voters from the electoral market actually benefit the power and position of governing parties. Therefore, voters' dissatisfaction with mainstream politics does not always lead to their 'voicing' protest that would trigger electoral change and the success of new parties (Tavits 2006, 2008), but also to their 'exiting' the electoral market (see, for instance, Morlino & Raniolo 2017, pp. 43–44).

We can glean a better understanding of this phenomenon by looking into party mobilisation strategies and how these stimulate voting (Karp & Banducci 2007). Certainly people who do not vote tend to have little contact with agencies of mobilisation (Brady, Verba & Schlozman 1995; Magalhães, Aldrich & Gibson 2020). Yet major parties are more effective in getting potential supporters to the polls as they tend to have more resources to do so; as a result, the people who do come to the polls tend to vote for them, while those who stay at home might be more likely to prefer smaller parties. In fact, empirical studies have shown that smaller parties benefit from increased turnout levels (Bernhagen & Marsh 2007).

This discussion is essential to understand the Portuguese case. Earlier studies have shown that voters dissatisfied with mainstream parties usually refrain from voting (Freire & Magalhães 2002; Freire 2001) and recent contributions observe that whereas discontented voters voted for radical and anti-party movements in Spain, Greece and Ireland, a significant proportion of the Portuguese voters decided not to vote at all in the elections held during the Great Recession (Raimundo & Pinto 2014). By exiting the electoral market, alienated Portuguese electors that are disenchanted with mainstream parties 'ironically give a stronger role to the moderate electors who participate and consequently strengthen the traditional parties that they despise' (Morlino & Raniolo 2017, pp. 27–28).

Abstentionists certainly do not form a homogenous group (e.g. de Sá 2009) and there are spatial variations in the effects of abstention on voting patterns (Garcia 2014; Freire & Magalhães 2002; Freire 2001). Yet the marginal success of new parties in Portugal, which we discuss in more detail later, suggests that most voters not do not see them as viable alternatives to the mainstream parties. Building on this debate, our expectation is that the vote for mainstream parties is associated with high abstention rates, while smaller parties tend to benefit from higher mobilisation levels (i.e. higher turnout).

The supply-side argument builds on the party strategy literature, in particular on the idea that party system change is fostered not only by voter-party alignments, but also by the strategies employed by political parties to gather popular support (Sitter 2002; Tromp 1989; Mair 1997). There are multiple strategies which may be combined (more or less successfully) in different ways. For instance, issue and credit claiming theories provide key arguments on how parties' behaviour impacts party system change. On the one hand, the issue-yield theory assumes that parties act strategically by emphasising those issues that will give them a competitive advantage, and ultimately increase their re-election odds (van Ditmars, Maggini & van Spanje 2020). Along this line, it has been shown that mainstream parties can change the salience and ownership of certain issues – either through accommodative or adversarial strategies – to avoid new party entry (Meguid 2005). On the other, credit claiming strategies refer to how politicians take credit for their success and thus convey a message that they are worthy of being re-elected (Twight 1991). These strategies may include maximising the positive impact of their own actions, but also trying to capitalise on events for which they were not directly responsible. Finally, the success of challenger parties seems to be associated with a communication strategy that strongly relies on the web and social networks (e.g. Mosca & Quaranta 2017).

In the Portuguese case, the analysis will focus on strategies of credit claiming that allowed the PS to regain its centrality in the party system and demarcate itself from its partners of the radical left. This strategy ultimately paid off electorally, thereby generating more predictable patterns of competition. The rightist parties were less effective in their strategies, notably by being incapable of highlighting electorally relevant issues, thereby leaving some space available for the emergence of new alternatives. As a result, we underline the mechanisms that allow the (marginal) success of new parties, namely the emphasis on new issues and campaign innovation.

Data and methods

We develop two empirical analyses to test the demand and supply-side explanations of party system change. The first tests the effect of turnout on the vote for major and smaller parties in the 2015 and 2019 elections. It draws on official estimates of turnout and vote for each party, disaggregated at the district and municipal levels. Between these two elections, a change was made to the electoral law (Law no. 47/2018) that gave Portuguese emigrants automatic access to the electoral roll, therefore artificially increasing the number of registered voters (Cancela & Vicente 2019, p. 81). Our analysis only considers national constituencies, i.e. 20 districts and 308 municipalities.

Turnout is the key independent variable and is measured as the percentage of voters given the population eligible to vote in each district/municipality (see Table A1 in the online appendix available here at https://doi.org/10.1080/13608746.2020.1862498: for descriptive statistics). The dependent variables measure the vote for major and smaller parties. In both the 2015 and 2019 elections, we consider PS and PSD as major parties since they secure the majority of votes and seats in parliament. Smaller parties are all others that managed to elect a candidate; in 2015 they include the BE, CDU (the electoral coalition between PCP and PEV) and the PAN, and in 2019 the BE, CDS-PP, CH, IL, L, PAN and CDU.[2] We start by performing multilevel models with fixed effects at the municipal level to estimate the impact of turnout on the vote for major and smaller parties. The models also control for district magnitude as it has been demonstrated that abstention and voting opportunities vary according to district size (Garcia 2014). We then present a set of maps displaying the geographic relationship between turnout and voting behaviour.

The second empirical analysis tests the leverage of supply side factors, and more specifically party strategy, to understand the incremental changes observed in the Portuguese party system between 2015 and 2019. To do so, we rely on several sources of qualitative data such as the usage of online tools, news in the media, and selected campaign messages. The data aim to shed light on the strategies used by the PS and how this constrained the competition and room for manoeuvre of radical left parties that supported the cabinet. It also reveals the limited success of right-wing parties' strategies and how new parties took advantage of various mechanisms to enter parliament.

Before presenting the findings of the empirical analysis, the next section contextualises the Portuguese party system since democratisation. The goal is to clarify patterns of change and continuity over time, but more importantly to demonstrate – based on several indicators – that post-bailout elections did not engender significant and sustained change in the basic rules of interparty competition.

The evolution of the Portuguese party system over the democratic period

This section examines the Portuguese party system before and after the bailout period. Before a more in-depth analysis of party system dynamics, we briefly introduce the main political protagonists. Four parties have largely dominated the political scene since Portuguese democracy was established in 1974: two mainstream parties (the centre left PS and the centre right PSD), plus two smaller forces (the extreme left PCP and the right-wing CDS-PP). The BE, a left-libertarian movement party has also been a regular presence in parliament since its foundation in 1999.

Ideological heterogeneity and flexibility are the main characteristics of the PSD, and more so than of the PS. These two centrist parties have led every government since democratisation. They are generally characterised as catch-all parties, with party leadership playing a strong role, especially in terms of strategy and the recruitment process. This also applies to the CDS-PP, which can be considered more a cadre party, while the PCP still displays many features associated with orthodox communist parties.

During the democratic period, the main change in the Portuguese party system took place between the elections of 1985 and 1987 with the meteoric rise of a new party, the Democratic Renewal Party (PRD, *Partido Renovador Democrático*), which was able to achieve the third position in the party system. However, its sudden fall led to a bipolarisation trend, majoritarian dynamics and the alternation of PS and PSD in government. As several studies have shown, economic issues have played an overwhelming role in structuring the content and dynamics of the political space in Portugal (Ferreira da Silva & Mendes 2019; Tsatsanis, Freire & Tsirbas 2014). This (quasi)unidimensional pattern of inter-party competition has remained relatively stable and was only at times counter-balanced by election-specific issues, while no new cleavages have been politicised (see also Lisi 2019).

A closer examination of the recent evolution of the Portuguese party system is based on several indicators measured since democratic transition. In Table 1, the effective number of electoral parties (ENEP) and the number of parliamentary parties (ENPP) serve as indicators of fragmentation, while electoral volatility illustrates the degree of (in)stability in the patterns of interparty competition. This is complemented by raw electoral data (see Table 2) that depict the percentage of seats/votes of both the major parties and the new parties, and a classification of cabinet types over time.

During the first decade of the democratic regime, the level of fragmentation was relatively low (average 3.5 between 1976 and 1985). After the electoral realignment that took place between 1985 and 1987, the number of parties was further diminished due to the trend towards majoritarian patterns that emerged

Table 1. Party system indicators: Portugal (1975–2019).

	ENEP	ENPP	TV	BV	IV
1975	4.2	2.9	-	-	-
1976	4.4	3.4	8.4	5.2	3.2
1979	3.4	2.8	8.7	4.3	4.4
1980	3.3	2.8	3.0	1.2	1.8
1983	3.9	3.4	10.7	6.8	3.9
1985	5.0	4.2	21.4	0.4	21
1987	2.4	2.4	22.1	14.9	7.2
1991	2.8	2.2	8.7	1.7	7.0
1995	3.1	2.6	19.2	13.6	5.6
1999	3.2	2.6	2.5	2.0	0.5
2002	3.1	2.6	8.5	7.9	0.6
2005	3.3	2.6	12.5	12.1	0.4
2009	4.1	3.1	8.1	4.0	4.1
2011	4.0	2.9	12.6	12	0.6
2015	3.7	2.7	13.8	11.8	2.0
2019	4.4	2.9	8.5	7.8	0.7

Source: Authors' elaboration with data from Ministry of Internal Administration, MAI-DGAI.

Note: ENEP (Effective Number of Electoral Party); ENPP (Effective Number of Parliamentary Parties); TV (Total Volatility); BV (bloc Volatility).

after the 1990s (Table 1). Indeed, with the exception of the PRD, there have been very few cases of new party entry in the Portuguese Parliament, generally limited to one party that gathers a very small fraction of seats (always in Lisbon, the largest district).[3] Yet it should be noted that there has been an increase in the number of political parties since the 2002 elections. The number of new parties increased slightly after 2009, oscillating between three and five (the peak achieved in the 2011 elections). Despite the large number of parties running for the first time at elections, their electoral results have never been influential and have had no significant impact on party system dynamics, even though it proved difficult for the two mainstream parties to retain widespread support and provide stable government solutions.

Overall, the average total volatility (TV) for the period between 1976 and 2019 is 11.4, which is quite low when compared for instance with South European countries (Sanches 2021). This indicator peaked in elections marked by the rise of new forces (1985 and 1987) but, for the most part and particularly since the 1990s, it expresses vote shifts between the two mainstream parties (e.g. 1995). This pattern is linked to the weak societal roots of moderate parties and the role of contextual factors in the voting choice of centrist voters (e.g. Gunther & Montero 2001; Jalali 2007; Lisi 2019).

This finding is also confirmed when we look at bloc volatility (BV), which measures vote shifts between two ideological blocs. Indeed, most of the volatility is based on electoral shifts between mainstream left-wing and right-wing parties, which suggests a relatively high permeability of moderate voters that punish incumbents by voting for the main opposition party, thus reinforcing a two-party dynamics. Regarding the evolution of volatility before and after the crisis, the figures indicate remarkable stability. The average volatility of the two pre-crisis elections (2002 and 2005) was approximately 10, which corresponds to the volatility scores during the crisis (2009 and 2011). Total volatility goes up slightly to 11 in post-troika elections (2015 and 2019), but the highest value (13.8) is still quite low and far from the abrupt electoral changes recorded in other European countries in the last decade (see Chiaramonte & Emanuele 2017).

Finally, it is important to recall Mair's (1997) notion of structures of competition in order to examine the degree of continuity and change in the party system with regard to the governmental arena. As noted by a number of authors (Jalali 2018; Bertoa 2019), the Portuguese party system has been characterised by the rapid closure of its structure of competition, with the composition of governments based on the same three governing parties (PS, PSD and CDS-PP). After the 1990s, single-party governments replaced coalition governments, and governing formulas started to display familiar patterns (see Table 2). The main change in this arena occurred after the 2015 elections with the emergence of a new government formula known as '*Geringonça*' (literally 'Contraption') which will be detailed in the coming pages. However, this arrangement was led by PS and had a temporary character as it did not survive after the 2019 elections. This ephemeral fluctuation in the governmental arena was not enough to change the Portuguese party system, which maintained a relatively high degree of institutionalisation. In order words, by and large Portuguese politics continues to be structured by the mainstream centre-left /centre-right parties.

The 2015 and 2019 legislative elections in Portugal: between continuity and innovation

The Great Recession led to some changes, albeit minor, in the Portuguese party system. On the one hand, it created the necessary conditions for a unique event in the history of Portuguese democracy (Sanches 2021; Jalali 2019; Lisi 2016; Fernandes, Magalhães & Santana-Pereira 2018), namely the negotiation of a new governing formula between the PS and the two radical left parties (BE and PCP) after the 2015 elections. This was triggered by the fact that neither of the two largest parties, or coalitions, had a majority in the parliament. On the other hand, although new political parties entered the parliament in the 2015 and 2019 elections, they mostly elected few candidates. Next, we examine the patterns of continuity and change in the Portuguese party system – in the electoral, parliamentary and governmental arenas – in the last two elections.

The electoral arena

To a great extent, the 2015 elections were 'normal' elections that produced unexpected results. The two main parties – plus the CDS-PP, which ran in coalition with the PSD – obtained slightly less than 70 per cent of the votes, while the two radical left parties received the support of approximately 18 per cent of the electorate. Electoral volatility was quite low, and it was mostly based on bloc volatility, i.e. shifts between the right bloc and the PS. Only PAN benefited from the loss of popularity of mainstream parties, obtaining 1.39 per cent of the votes and electing one MP for the first time.

The 2019 elections had elements of both continuity and change. On the one hand, the two-party format of the Portuguese system again proved to be consolidated at its core: taken together, the two main parties polled 64.6 per cent of the votes and got 81 per cent of the potential parliamentary seats. It is worth noting that the steady decrease in terms of the absolute number of votes for the two main parties between the 2009 and 2019 elections (see Table 2) did not change the trend that dates back to the 1990 of the two main governing parties being able to maintain a majoritarian position in the Parliament despite having fewer votes.

On the other hand, new parties entered the parliament and there was a significant realignment of voting on the right of the political spectrum.

Newcomers include L on the left side, the IL on the right and the CH on the radical right. Each on its own terms, these new parties represented alternative views on European integration and globalisation conflicts that were outside of the traditional party offer. Innovation thus came from the right of the political spectrum in particular. First the CDS-PP and the PSD lost support in these elections. The CDS-PP experienced its worst result since 1987, consolidating the party's underwhelming results in the May European parliamentary elections. The PSD also had one of its worst performances in legislative elections mirroring, among other things, the lack of internal cohesion and higher factionalism. These vote shifts led to a substantial increase in the ENEP, which reached the score of 4.4, the highest value since the major party system realignment in the 1980s. This is also confirmed if we look at the vote in extra-parliamentary parties, which enjoyed increased support in the last two elections compared to the previous period (see Table 2). The last two elections also recorded the highest number of genuinely new parties, with four and five new parties contesting the legislative election in 2015 and 2019, respectively.

Continuity also characterises the content and dynamics of patterns of competition in the last two elections. In 2015, the impact of the bailout led to a higher polarisation of the political space around the dimension that has dominated electoral alignments, namely the economy (Ferreira da Silva & Mendes 2019, pp. 154–156). The changing economic environment in 2019 contributed to a more diversified campaign agenda (see Fernandes & Magalhães 2020), but the main issues that shaped the political space were still structured along the left-right divide (e.g. public services) and no new cultural issues were emphasised, in particular by the main political actors or the media (see Carvalho & Duarte 2020).

The temporal patterns of electoral volatility further underscore the moderate changes experienced in Portugal. In fact, while total volatility increased between 2009 and 2015, it is still quite low relative to values registered in Europe during the crisis period. The 2011 and 2015 elections resulted in government alternation between the two main moderate forces, while the 2019 elections saw a slight decrease in volatility scores. Yet these elections also brought some new dynamics to the fore, especially in terms of new parties. First, PAN experienced growing national support, increasing its support in most districts, especially among younger and more educated voters.[4] Second, L and IL appealed to individuals with higher levels of education and income, particularly in the most populated districts (Lisbon and Oporto). Finally, CH received a remakably uniform support, spread equally across districts with higher and lower population density. Although its electoral success was in part due to the CDS-PP's disastrous performance, its anti-establishment rhetoric may have mobilised new voters or attracted voters from both centrist and even leftist areas. More importantly, CH's electoral base shows stark differences from that of the extreme-right PNR (*Partido Nacional Renovador*, Renewal National Party), which suggests it was

Table 2. Vote patterns and types of cabinet in Portugal (1975–2019).

Year	Vote concentration (PS+PSD)	Vote concentration % (PS+PSD)	Seats concentration % (PS+PSD)	Vote for new parties %	Seats for new parties	Vote for extra-parliamentary parties	Cabinet type
1975	3,670,254	64.3	68.4	-	-	497.996	Minority single party (PS)
1976	3,248,302	59.2	59.6	1.87	0	312.626	Minority coalition (PS/CDS-PP)
1979	4,361,344	72.9	59.2	2.5	1	222.231	Majority coalition (PSD/CDS-PP)
1980	4,541,375	71.6	70.4	1.2	0	337.853	Majority coalition (PSD/CDS-PP)
1983	3,616,113	63.4	58.0	0.4	0	196.498	Minority coalition (PS/PSD)
1985	2,936,609	50.6	83.2	18.1	45	202.247	Minority single party (PSD)
1987	4,113,290	72.5	90.0	0	0	219.715	Majority single party (PSD)
1991	4,573,109	79.7	87.0	1.7	1	196.654	Majority single party (PSD)
1995	4,598,344	77.9	85.2	0.3	0	152.790	Minority single party (PS)
1999	4,136,080	76.4	87.4	2.6	0	98.507	Minority single party (PS)
2002	4,269,349	78.0	85.2	0.1	0	87.095	Majority coalition (PSD/CDS-PP)
2005	4,241,737	73.8	77.4	0.7	0	121.117	Majority single party (PS)
2009	3,730,903	66.8	79.1	1.1	0	176.258	Minority single party (PS)
2011	3,725,528	65.7	76.1	1.5	0	247.499	Majority coalition (PSD/CDS-PP)
2015	3,741,606	70.9	81.3	3.2	1	392.792	Contract parliamentarism (PS/PCP, PEV, LB)
2019	3,365,740	64.6		4.2	3	208.284	Minority single party (PS)
Pre-bailout elections	3,728,215	66.3	78.3	1.3	0	211.879	
Post-bailout elections	3,553,673	67.8	78.7	3.7	2	300.538	

1) in some elections (1979, 1980, 2015) PSD and CDS-PP formed a pre-electoral coalition. 2) new parties are considered those brand-new forces that run for the first time in legislative elections. 3) pre-bailout elections include the 2009 and 2011 contests; post-bailout elections are the 2015 and 2019 legislative elections.

Source: Authors' elaboration with data from CNE and MAI (Ministry of Internal Administration). Cabinet type information was extracted from Jalali (2017, p. 76).

able to appeal to voters with a less clear ideological profile. Overall, these changes are not sufficient to allow us to speak of a change in the trend observed in the party system since 1987, in which the two main parties (PS and PSD) retain enough electoral support to remain crucial actors in electoral competition and in parliament.

The parliamentary and governmental arenas

While continuity is the main trend of the party system at the electoral level, the findings in the parliamentary arena are mixed. In order to examine patterns of change and continuity in this arena of competition, we rely on three distinct indicators. The first is the concentration of seats in the two main parties, compared to the proportion of votes obtained by PS and PSD together (see Table 2). From this viewpoint, it is worth noting that the decrease in vote concentration that started in 2005 did not produce an erosion of parliamentary seats of the same magnitude. This is understandable due to the distortion of the electoral system, which tends to favour bigger parties (see more details in the next section).

The second piece of evidence is based on the ENPP. Also in this case, the evolution of ENPP does not accompany the increase in party system fragmentation registered at the electoral level. ENPP oscillated between 2.7 and 2.9 in the last two elections (Table 1), below the peak reached in the 2009 elections (3.1). Indeed, continuity clearly prevails in the parliamentary arena vis-à-vis patterns of change. This means that during the crisis, there was growing divergence between the trend registered at the electoral level, on the one hand, and the evolution of parliamentary dynamics, on the other.

However, if we consider the third indicator, namely the number of parliamentary groups and the number of new MPs, the picture shows that something changed after the 2015 elections. As noted before, the innovation was very modest in 2015 with one new MP from PAN being elected. However, in the 2019 legislative elections, both the number of parliamentary groups and of new MPs (i.e. MPs elected in new parties) rose substantially (from six to nine and from one to three, respectively). The numbers do not allow for relevant changes in terms of inter-party competition or the functioning of the parliament, but they are nonetheless a break vis-à-vis the past twenty years.

The last arena of party interaction is that of the government. Although government composition and innovation were characterised by no change, the formula of the new government formed after the 2015 elections represented a 'turning point' in the Portuguese party system. These elections produced an unexpected outcome due to the decision of the left-wing parties (plus the Greens) to agree to support a socialist government. The point that is worth stressing is that the so-called 'Geringonça' was an invention of party leaders and this was the most important driver of party system change. Nevertheless, the unprecedented degree of cooperation between left-wing forces did not produce systematic and lasting changes. The *'Geringonça'* was the result of a unique set of circumstances and it was not accompanied by significant changes in the electoral or parliamentary arenas (Jalali 2018).

Explaining party system change and continuity in Portugal

The literature on party system change does not seem to fully account for more deviant cases such as Portugal. First, although it was one of the countries most severely affected by the Great Recession, economic factors are unable to explain the evolution of the Portuguese party system. Second, institutional barriers have basically remained the same throughout the democratic period. Third, voters have not relied massively on protest to voice their dissatisfaction with existing alternatives. Consequently, this study relies on understudied aspects based on both a demand-side and a supply-side perspective in order to interpret party system change.

Abstention as a driver of party system inertia

Although Portuguese citizens value the electoral dimension of democracy (Gorbunova, Sanches & Lobo 2015), voters have gone less to the polls over the years (Cancela & Vicente 2019). Abstention was very low in the first democratic elections, but it increased significantly in the mid-1980s with the

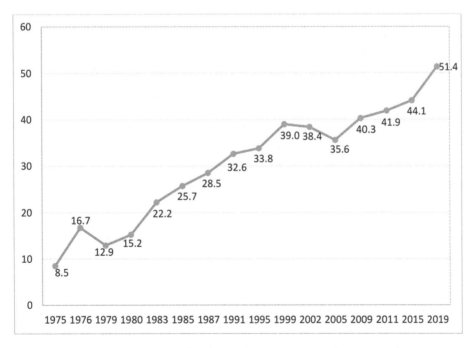

Figure 1. Evolution of abstention in legislative elections in Portugal (1975–2019).
Source: authors' elaboration from the data available in SGMAI and PORDATA.

consolidation of Portuguese democracy and the electoral realignment of 1985–1987 (Figure 1). In the 1990s abstention rates oscillated around one third of the electorate. After a slight decline in the early 2000s, abstention went up around 11 percentage points between 2009 and 2019. From a comparative perspective, the Portuguese case is striking for the intensity of turnout decline, which makes this case more similar to Eastern countries than Western democracies.

In the 2019 legislative elections, the scenario of low turnout was even worse than in the previous years. In comparison to the 2015 elections, abstention increased seven percentage points and was higher than in the local elections held in 2017. However, as Cancela & Vicente (2019) argue, this increase is somewhat artificial and is partly due to the automatic registration in electoral rolls since 2018 of Portuguese citizens residing abroad.[5] In fact, when we consider the estimates of voters with the right to vote (as opposed to registered voters), abstention essentially remained constant (Cancela & Vicente 2019, p. 23).

In order to investigate the effect of abstention on party system change (stability), we regress turnout rates at the municipal level with the votes obtained by political parties, controlling by district magnitude (see descriptive and regression results in Tables A1 and A2 in the appendix). The results for a linear mixed-effects model show a positive relationship between abstention and vote for major parties in both the 2015 and 2019 elections, whereas there is a negative relationship between abstention and vote for smaller parties. Turnout is only statistically significant to explain the vote for major and smaller parties in 2015 and, even though it does not reach significance in 2019, it goes in the hypothesised direction. Thus, overall, our expectations are confirmed given that high levels of abstention helped maintain the established position of the two major political parties in the party system, while penalising smaller parties.

Figure 2 displays the geographical relationship between turnout and vote for major and smaller parties. In the northeast of Portugal, where there is a higher rate of voter abstention, we observe a larger vote for major parties. PSD lost a significant part of its electoral stronghold in the north of Portugal in 2019, and PS was able to capture a large share of this: the majority of new municipalities gained by PS in 2019 in comparison with the 2015 elections were concentrated in this region. Hence, the two maps are not markedly different with regard to vote for major parties. In contrast, we see a larger vote for smaller parties in the south of the country, where abstention is relatively low. The electoral performance of the BE and especially the CH, which obtained an above average proportion of votes in the south in 2019, accounts for this thriving scenario for smaller parties in this region.

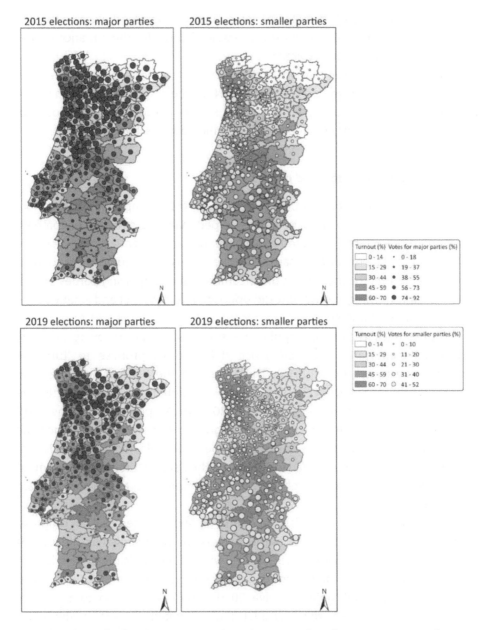

Figure 2. Relationship between turnout and vote in major and smaller parties in 2015 and 2019. *Source*: authors' elaboration from the data available in the General Secretariat of the Ministry of Internal Administration (SGAI-AE).

On the other hand, district magnitude, which we included as a control, does not display a significant effect in any of the models estimated (see Table A2 in the appendix). Notwithstanding, it should be noted that the effect is as expected, in that new parties are more likely to be elected in high district magnitudes. In fact, without exception, all new parties that entered parliament in the last two legislative elections were elected in the country's largest district

(Lisbon) by winning just over 22,000 votes. This corroborates the notion that the biggest districts provide the most favourable channel for the entrance of new parties in the parliamentary arena.

These findings reveal that abstention can be an important element feeding the inertia of the Portuguese party system. Nevertheless, other aspects might be relevant to explain the vote for major and smaller parties, such as sociodemographic factors or party-related variables, which deserve further research.

The strategies of established parties

Elections in the post-bailout period were marked by competition being more structured around two blocs. While this helped make the structure of competition more predictable, it created new challenges and potentially compromised the image and identity of the parties involved. Thus, after four years of contract parliamentarism, to what extent did incumbent and supporting parties benefit from their governing status? How did opposition forces react and what was the strategy of newcomers?

With a track record of popular measures, economic recovery and low unemployment rates, the *Geringonça* delivered its promise to 'turn the page on austerity' (Costa 2015). This benefited the PS, first and foremost, as shown by growing levels of approval (see Botelho 2019) – trust in the government rose from 18 per cent in 2015 to 42 per cent in June 2019 (Eurobarometer). During the 2019 campaign, the PS successfully claimed the government had been responsible for the economic recovery, while the radical left parties did not manage to frame their support for the government as a success story, but merely as one of compromise to advance certain policy goals.

The leader of the communists (Jerónimo de Sousa) stated that 'all progress, all policies [approved] in favour of the workers and the people had the imprint of the PCP and the Greens' (TSF 2019), while Catarina Martins, BE's leader, claimed that her party had been proactive and most of all a 'stabilising force' against an often inflexible PS (Silva 2019). António Costa, in turn, skilfully demarcated the PS from the radical left and presented the party as the dominant force in the governing solution. The radical left parties found themselves in a difficult position. On the one hand, they approved most legislation proposed by the executive and sought to take credit for the perceived success (De Giorgi & Cancela 2019). On the other hand, by supporting the cabinet they may have compromised their ideological image. Overall, the *Geringonça* benefited the PS while it simultaneously helped demobilise potential opposition on the left. The electoral results suggest a possible transfer of votes from the PCP and the BE to the PS in key strongholds (Fernandes & Magalhães 2020). In this sense, the PS strategy strengthened its dominance in the Portuguese party system and engendered more predictable patterns of competition.

On the other side of the ideological spectrum, the right-wing parties – PSD and CDS-PP – were unable to exploit popular dissatisfaction or politicise new issues to gain support. The PSD leader lacked a clear strategy. During the campaign, Rui Rio admitted the possibility of a coalition with the usual partner CDS-PP after elections, but at the same time he did not set aside collaborating with the PS on issues of national interest. In addition, the PSD failed to successfully articulate and communicate the main policy goals, and it was not able to demarcate itself from its direct competitor. The CDS-PP leader tried to claim the conservative vote and the rightist electorate left void by the PSD. However, this move raised further intraparty instability and in the end it was unable to conquer PSD sympathisers or to mobilise new voters. Overall, the right-wing parties' strategy was ineffective and negatively impacted their electoral performance, while paving the way for the emergence of new political actors.

The strategies of new parties

Whereas established Portuguese parties largely define the content of political debate, emerging parties have relied on new issues – that were not part of the traditional left-right offer – as part of their strategy to reach the parliament. Arguably, the most successful case was the breakthrough in 1999 of the BE, which demarcated itself from existing parties on the left (PS and PCP) by its emphasis on post-materialist issues, a critique of European integration and the adoption of a more participatory and deliberative organisational model. More than a decade later, in 2015, it would be the PAN – a niche party focusing on environmental issues – that would enter parliament. Although the PEV had been taking a position on environmental issues for decades, its public image was somewhat overshadowed by its long-time coalition partner (PCP). In contrast, the PAN was able to successfully articulate a climate crisis message and to capitalise on the increasing global and national concern about environmental issues.

In 2019, the three new parties that appeared on the parliamentary scene – the rightist IL, the far-right populist CH, and the ecological, libertarian and pro-European L – were also able to take advantage of neglected issues. The IL presented a far more liberal economic agenda than the PSD and CDS-PP. The L, a pro-European left-libertarian party, distanced itself the most from other left-wing parties by its focus on gender and racial equality issues (Fernandes & Magalhães 2020). Finally, the CH emphasised an anti-establishment message and crime and security agenda (Mendes & Dennison 2020). Among other things, the party 'pledged to suppress gender quotas for political offices, and to support chemical castration for sex offenders and harsher sentencing for corruption cases, the elimination of corporate income taxes for small business owners, and the immediate deportation of all illegal immigrants' (Fernandes & Magalhães 2020, p. 4).

The second aspect to be highlighted is that the use of new technologies might have favoured new party entry, particularly those parties with fewer resources. In 2015, despite being small and relatively unknown, the PAN was the second highest party (after the PSD) in terms of 'likers/friends' and user engagement on Facebook, and it exhibited the biggest growth in terms of likes (Serra-Silva, Carvalho & Fazendeiro 2018). Fast-forward to 2019 and it is interesting to note that some of these trends were accentuated. The IL, CH and PAN – and in part the L – are the parties whose share of followers on Facebook and Twitter (as percentage of voters) is the highest, while the PS and the PSD have the lowest share of followers on both platforms (Figure 3). The PSD is the only traditional and more established party investing in social media on multiple fronts (YouTube; Twitter; Instagram; Pinterest; Flickr). The technological divide that we observe in the Portuguese party system, opposing newer to older parties (with the partial exception of the PSD), can be explained by the fact that these emerging parties came to the fore in a new technological era where mastering online communication is critical to their mobilisation strategy; this is particularly important due to the closed nature of the Portuguese party system, for example in terms of (mainstream) political communication, party funding and patterns of competition (Salgado 2019; Serra-Silva, Carvalho & Fazendeiro 2018).[6]

The third and final aspect is the campaign strategies. The IL presented outstanding and original campaign material. The party's billboards were provocative

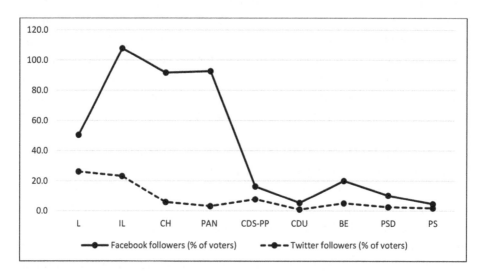

Figure 3. Portuguese parties' followers on Facebook and Twitter as of November 2019 (% of 2019 voters).
Source: Authors' elaboration.
Note: The percentage of Facebook and Twitter followers is calculated given the total number of votes received by each party. For example, the PS polled 1,908,036 votes, and has 87,454 followers in Facebook (4.6 per cent of voters) and 34,302 in Twitter (1.8 per cent of voters).

and ironic, and positioned at strategic points of the city, including next to the PS billboards. Another original initiative was the sending of letters to citizens that simulated the lettering of the Tax Authority. Letters were sent to nearly 200,000 citizens and the first two lines read 'Dear taxpayer. Don't be afraid. This time it is not from the tax authorities', and went on to say, 'Portuguese citizens live under the rule of a state that takes months to pay off its debts but does not hesitate to use disproportionate methods to collect taxpayers' debts' (Correira 2019). Rodrigo Saraiva from the IL, who is also an expert in advertising and communication strategies, explained in an interview that the party wanted to make a difference (Correira 2019). Thus, after the European elections they selected the councils and parishes in which the party had received most votes and sent the letter to residents in these places.

In the case of CH, the party leader André Ventura also made skilful use of social media, spreading controversial campaign messages and pictures. However, his regular presence in traditional media may have had a greater impact on raising his visibility. A former member of the PSD, Ventura defected from the party after Rui Rio's election as party leader in 2018 and became notorious not only for his anti-system and politically incorrect statements, but especially for acting as a football pundit for a private channel, CMTV, which currently has the highest share of viewers. The focus on other salient issues besides immigration allows this new force to avoid the stigma traditionally associated with radical right forces, although the party did not benefit from an opening of the opportunity structure – in contrast to the Spanish *Vox* – because sociocultural issues have displayed a low salience (see Mendes & Dennison 2020).

The L innovated by being the only party to organise primaries to select candidates to parliament and also by the kind of issues they presented, namely combining a strong ecological and identity agenda with a clear pro-European stance. Its presence in social media was also noteworthy, particularly on Twitter, and it tried to concentrate its mobilisation effort primarily in bigger constituencies.

Overall, not only is the Portuguese case revealing of how challenger parties can attract voter support through the formulation of innovative issues and a strategic use of campaign communication strategies, but it also reveals how mainstream parties can constrain or accelerate party system change. These are the two sides of the same coin, which account for the gradual (or 'surreptitious', see Ferreira da Silva & Mendes 2019) change. In fact, new parties face a well-established party system with a closed structure of competition, anchored in government alternation between the two ideological blocs, thus limiting the potential innovation in the electoral arena.

Conclusions

The aim of this study was to examine patterns of change and continuity in the Portuguese party system. We took Portugal as a deviant case to understand the puzzle of party system change more broadly, given two particular features. On the one hand, Portugal diverges from other Southern European countries, which have been characterised by 'electoral catharsis' that completely reshaped party system configurations. In fact, what we observe is a pattern of incremental change which has not affected the 'core' of the party system. On the other, the interpretation of party system dynamics in the last decade notes the important role played by voter mobilisation and party strategies, vis-à-vis concurrent explanations such as economic performance and the design of political institutions, more generally.

The multi-dimensional analysis of the Portuguese party system shows that the degree of change before and after the crisis was limited. In fact, there is still a fair amount of predictability in electoral competition despite fluctuation in electoral support, a new governing formula in 2015 and the emergence of new political parties in 2019. By and large, the two mainstream parties remain pivotal, and virtually the only ones with credible expectations of forming a government. Therefore, we concur with Ferreira da Silva and Mendes (2019, p. 163) that the limited changes have less to do with major shifts in voter-party alignments than with party-induced transformations.

We then performed two empirical analyses to understand the patterns of change and continuity in the Portuguese party system in the post bailout period. In the first, we tested a demand-side explanation, i.e. the effect of turnout on voting behaviour, using data on the 2015 and 2019 elections disaggregated at the district and municipal level. The results gave some support to our expectations as major parties tend to obtain a higher proportion of votes in contexts of low turnout, while smaller parties benefit from higher levels of turnout. Even though the models could be improved by including more variables, the results are telling insofar as they confirm earlier studies on the topic (Freire & Magalhães 2002; Freire 2001) and the party and voting behaviour literature (Katz & Mair 2018, 1995). The second analysis examined a supply-side explanation, namely the role of party strategies in shaping the outcome of elections and inter-party competition. The results revealed how new issues, innovative campaign strategies and tools helped smaller parties to gain representation. However, the overall scenario reflects the strong gatekeeping capacity of major parties. Not only do they enjoy a natural advantage in terms of funding and organisational capacity, but they also quite successfully cover the left-right dimension which is the main axis of party competition in Portugal.

These results inform our understanding of the way party systems gradually adapt and evolve, but they also have wider implications for our comprehension of the transformation of voter-party linkages and democratic political representation. Our findings suggest that, in an environment characterised by the growing use of digital technology, mounting levels of abstention and wide disaffection, it is easier for new parties to break the threshold of representation.

In other words, the context in which party competition takes place provides powerful incentives for new challenger parties to engage successfully in the electoral arena. These phenomena are likely to increase party system instability in the foreseeable future, even for highly institutionalised party systems like that of Portugal.

There are, of course, other factors that contribute to understanding the functioning of the Portuguese party system, namely trust in political institutions, short-term policy evaluations, historical legacies and increased cartelisation of political parties (Bertoa 2019; Jalali 2018, 2019; Sanches 2021; Jalali, Silva & Silva 2012). Future studies may want to expand on the issues raised in this article and to examine the phenomenon of party system change beyond the limitations of this study. This study has taken a narrow approach by focusing on a single country, but comparative works are certainly welcome if we are to achieve more robust conclusions. Another avenue for further research may be an examination of voter-party alignments, following the traditional cleavage approach. Future studies may want to look more systematically at the electoral geography of party competition, testing more variables and for a longer period. Further analyses may also choose to focus on the electoral bases of new parties, especially if they are able to consolidate their institutional position.

Notes

1. 'Contract parliamentarism' can be defined as a publicly written agreement that establishes a contract between the minority government and the parties outside the cabinet, for more than a short-period or specific policy deal (Bale & Bergman 2006).
2. A more detailed description of both the dependent and independent variables is provided in the online appendix.
3. UDP (*União Democrática Popular*, Popular Democratic Union) and PSN (*Partido da Solidariedade Nacional*, National Solidarity Party) also elected one MP each in the Lisbon constituency in the 1979 and 1991 legislative elections, respectively.
4. See *Expresso*, 12 October 2019, p. 33.
5. It is important to note that unlike citizens residing in the home country, emigrants are not obliged to register, mainly because it is hard to monitor electoral registration abroad. Since 2018 citizens living abroad are automatically registered when they obtain the Citizens Card.
6. See Figure A1 in the online appendix for an idea of the inequalities in terms of campaign budget.

Acknowledgments

The authors would like to thank José Santana Pereira and Elisabetta Di Giorgi, for organizing the special issue, and for the comments made on the initial versions of this paper. We are also indebted to the journal's editors and to two anonymous reviewers for their careful reading and insightful comments. This study was supported by the *Fundação para a Ciência e Tecnologia* (FCT), grant number PTDC/IVC-CPO/1864/2014.

Disclosure statement

No potential conflict of interest was reported by the author(s).

Funding

This study was supported by the *Fundação para a Ciência e Tecnologia* (FCT), grant number PTDC/IVC-CPO/1864/2014.

ORCID

Marco Lisi ⓘ http://orcid.org/0000-0001-9833-0347
Edalina Rodrigues Sanches ⓘ http://orcid.org/0000-0001-6007-3680
Jayane dos Santos Maia ⓘ http://orcid.org/0000-0002-7877-2057

References

Bale, T. & Bergman, T. (2006) 'Captives no longer, but servants still? Contract parliamentarism and the new minority governance in Sweden and New Zealand', *Government and Opposition*, vol. 41, no. 3, pp. 422–449.

Bernhagen, P. & Marsh, M. (2007) 'Voting and protesting: Explaining citizen participation in old and new European democracies', *Democratisation*, vol. 14, no. 1, pp. 44–72.

Bertoa, F. C. (2019) 'The calm before the storm: explaining the institutionalization of Southern European party systems before the great recession', *European Politics and Society*, vol. 20, no. 5, pp. 567–590.

Bértoa, F. C. (2018) 'The three waves of party system institutionalisation studies: a multi- or uni-dimensional concept?', *Political Studies Review*, vol. 16, no. 1, pp. 60–72.

Botelho, L. (2019) 'Maioria quer que PS governe, mesmo que não ganhe as legislativas', *Público*, 22 May. https://www.publico.pt/2019/05/22/politica/noticia/maioria-quer-ps-governe-nao-ganhe-legislativas-1873608.

Brady, H. E., Verba, S. & Schlozman, K. L. (1995) 'Beyond Ses: a resource model of political participation', *The American Political Science Review*, vol. 89, no. 2, pp. 271–294.

Broughton, D. & Donovan, M. (Eds) (1998) *Changing Party Systens in Western Europe*, Pinter, London and New York.

Cancela, J. & Vicente, M. (2019) *Abstenção e Participação Eleitoral Em Portugal:Diagnóstico e Hipóteses de Reforma*, Câmara Municipal de Cascais, Cascais.

Carvalho, J. & Duarte, M. C. (2020) 'The politicization of immigration in Portugal between 1995 and 2014: a European exception?', *Journal of Common Market Studies*, vol. 58, no. 6, pp. 1469–1487.

Chiaramonte, A. & Emanuele, V. (2017) 'Party system volatility, regeneration and de-institutionalization in Western Europe (1945–2015)', *Party Politics*, vol. 23, no. 4, pp. 376–388.

Correia, J. D. (2019) 'Iniciativa Liberal envia 'carta' aos contribuintes: Não é preciso ter medo. Desta vez não é das Finanças', *Expresso*, 2 October. https://expresso.pt/legislativas-2019/2019-10-02-Iniciativa-Liberal-envia-carta-aos-contribuintes.-Nao-e-preciso-ter-medo.-Desta-vez-nao-e-das-Financas

Costa, A. (2015) 'Virar a página da austeridade, relançar a economia', *Jornal de Negócios*, 27 August https://www.jornaldenegocios.pt/opiniao/colunistas/detalhe/carta_de_antonio_costa_virar_a_pagina_da_austeridade_relancar_a_economia.

De Giorgi, E. & Cancela, J. (2019) 'The Portuguese radical left parties supporting government: from policy-takers to policymakers?', *Government and Opposition*, pp. 1–20. doi:10.1017/gov.2019.25.

De Giorgi, E. & Santana-Pereira, J. (2016) 'The 2015 Portuguese legislative election: widening the coalitional space and bringing the extreme left in', *South European Society & Politics*, vol. 21, no. 4, pp. 451–468.

de Sá, J. (2009) *Quem se abstém?* Campo da Comunicação, Lisbon.

Fernandes, J. & Magalhães, P. (2020) 'The 2019 Portuguese general elections', *West European Politics*, vol. 43, no. 4, pp. 1038–1050.

Fernandes, J. M., Magalhães, P. C. & Santana-Pereira, J. (2018) 'Portugal's leftist government: from sick man to poster boy?', *South European Society & Politics*, vol. 23, no. 4, pp. 503–524.

Ferreira da Silva, F. & Mendes, M. S. (2019) 'Portugal. A tale of apparent stability and surreptitious transformation', in *European Party Politics in Times of Crisis*, eds S. Hutter & H. Kriesi, Cambridge University Press, Cambridge, pp. 139–163.

Freire, A. (2001) *Mudança Eleitoral em Portugal: Clivagens, Economia e Voto em Eleições Legislativas 1983–1999*, Celta Editora, Lisbon.

Freire, A. & Magalhães, P. (2002) *Abstenção Eleitoral em Portugal*, Imprensa de Ciências Sociais, Lisbon.

Garcia, J. (2014) 'Determinants of electoral behavior: A study using individual-level data', MA thesis, Universidade Católica Portuguesa.

Gorbunova, E., Sanches, E. R. & Lobo, M. C. (2015) 'A satisfação com a democracia e os fatores explicativos. Portugal no contexto Europeu', in *Portugal Social em Mudança 2015*, eds J. Ferrão & A. Delicado, Imprensa de Ciências Sociais, Lisbon, pp. 9–17.

Gunther, R. & Montero, J. R. (2001) 'The anchors of partisanship', in *Parties, Politics, and Democracy in the New Southern Europe*, eds P. N. Diamandouros & R. Gunther, The Johns Hopkins University Press, Baltimore, pp. 83–152.

Hutter, S. & Kriesi, H. (2019) *European Party Politics in Times of Crisis*, Cambridge University Press, Cambridge.

Jalali, C. (2007) *Partidos e Democracia em Portugal 1974–2005*, Imprensa de Ciências Sociais, Lisbon.

Jalali, C. (2017), *Partidos e Sistemas Partidários*, Fundação Francisco Manuel dos Santos, Lisboa.

Jalali, C. (2018) 'The times (may) be a-changin'? The Portuguese party system in the twenty-first century', in *Party System Change, the European Crisis and the State of Democracy*, ed M. Lisi, Routledge, Abington, pp. 213–230.

Jalali, C. (2019) 'The Portuguese party system: evolution in continuity?', in *Political Institutions and Democracy in Portugal: Assessing the Impact of the Eurocrisis*, eds A. C. Pinto & C. P. Teixeira, Palgrave Macmillan, London, pp. 77–99.

Jalali, C., Silva, P. & Silva, S. (2012) 'Givers and takers: parties, state resources and civil society in Portugal', *Party Politics*, vol. 18, no. 61, pp. 61–80.

Karp, J. A. & Banducci, S. A. (2007) 'Party mobilization and political participation in new and old democracies', *Party Politics*, vol. 13, no. 2, pp. 217–234.

Katz, R. S. & Mair, P. (1995) 'Changing models of party organization and party democracy: the emergence of the cartel party', *Party Politics*, vol. 1, no. 1, pp. 5–28.

Katz, R. S. & Mair, P. (2018) *Democracy and the Cartelization of Political Parties*, Oxford University Press, Oxford.

Lago, I. & Martinez, F. (2010) 'Why new parties?', *Party Politics*, vol. 17, no. 1, pp. 3–20.

Lisi, M. (2016) 'U-turn: the Portuguese radical left from marginality to government support', *South European Society & Politics*, vol. 21, no. 4, pp. 541–560.

Lisi, M. (2019) *Eleições. Campanhas Eleitorais e Decisão de Voto em Portugal*, Edições Sílabo, Lisbon.

Magalhães, P., Aldrich, J. H. & Gibson, R. K. (2020) 'New forms of mobilization, new people mobilized? Evidence from the comparative study of electoral systems', *Party Politics*, vol. 26, no. 5, pp. 605–618.

Mainwaring, S. & Scully, T. R. (eds) (1995) *Building Democratic Institutions: Party Systems in Latin America*, Stanford University Press, Stanford.

Mainwaring, S. P. (1999) *Rethinking Party Systems in the Third Wave of Democratization*, Stanford University Press, Stanford.

Mair, P. (1989) 'The problem of party system change', *Journal of Theoretical Politics*, vol. 1, no. 3, pp. 251–276.

Mair, P. (1997) *Party System Change. Approaches and Interpretations*, Clarendon Press, London.

Meguid, B. M. (2005) 'Competition between unequals: the role of mainstream party strategy in niche party success', *American Political Science Review*, vol. 99, no. 3, pp. 347–359.

Mendes, M. S. & Dennison, J. (2020) 'Explaining the emergence of the radical right in Spain and Portugal: Salience, stigma and supply', *West European Politics*, pp. 1–24. doi:10.1080/01402382.2020.1777504.

Morlino, L. & Raniolo, F. (2017) *The Impact of the Economic Crisis on South European Democracies*, Palgrave MacMillan, London.

Mosca, L. & Quaranta, M. (2017) 'Voting for movement parties in Southern Europe: the role of protest and digital information', *South European Society & Politics*, vol. 22, no. 4, pp. 427–446.

Pedersen, M. N. (1990) 'Electoral volatility in Western Europe, 1948–1977', in *The West European Party System*, ed P. Mair, Oxford University Press, Oxford, pp. 195–208.

Pennings, P. & Lane, J.-E. (eds) (1998) *Comparing Party System Change*, Routledge, London.

Raimundo, F. & Pinto, A. Costa (2014) 'When parties succeed: Party system (in)stability and the 2008 financial crisis in Portugal', Paper presented at the 2014 Annual Meeting of the American Political Science Association, Washington DC, 28–31 August.

Salgado, S. (2019) 'Where's populism? Online media and the diffusion of populist discourses and styles in Portugal', *European Political Science*, vol. 18, no. 1, pp. 53–65.

Sanches, E. R. (2021) 'Party systems in comparative perspective', in *Varieties of Democracy in Southern Europe, 1960s-2000s: A Comparison between Spain, France, Greece, Italy and Portugal*, ed T. Fernandes, University of Notre Dame Press, Notre Dame (forthcoming).

Seawright, J. & Gerring, J. (2008) 'Case selection techniques in case study research: A menu of qualitative and quantitative options', *Political Research Quarterly*, vol. 61, no. 2, pp. 294–308.

Serra-Silva, S., Carvalho, D. D. & Fazendeiro, J. (2018) 'Party-citizen online challenges: Portuguese parties' Facebook usage and audience engagement', in *Citizenship in Crisis*, eds M. C. Lobo, F. C. da Silva & J. P. Zúquete, Imprensa de Ciências Sociais, Lisbon, pp. 185–214.

Silva, A. (2019) 'Catarina Martins responde a Costa: "O BE nunca contou com o PS para nada"', *Expresso*, 28 August https://expresso.pt/politica/2019-08-29-Catarina-Martins-responde -a-Costa-O-BE-nunca-contou-com-o-PS-para-nada.

Sitter, N. (2002) 'Cleavages, party strategy and party system change in Europe, East and West', *Perspectives on European Politics and Society*, vol. 3, no. 3, pp. 425–451.

Tavits, M. (2006) 'Party system change: testing a model of new party entry', *Party Politics*, vol. 12, no. 1, pp. 99–119.

Tavits, M. (2008) 'Party systems in the making: the emergence and success of new parties in new democracies', *British Journal of Political Science*, vol. 38, no. 1, pp. 113–133.

Tromp, B. (1989) 'Party strategies and system change in the Netherlands', *West European Politics*, vol. 12, no. 4, pp. 82–97.

Tsatsanis, E., Freire, A. & Tsirbas, Y. (2014) 'The impact of the economic crisis on the ideological space in Portugal and Greece: a comparison of elites and voters', *South European Society & Politics*, vol. 19, no. 4, pp. 519–540.

TSF (2019) 'Jerónimo acusa Costa de "enfeitar-se" com medidas da CDU a que se opôs', *TSF*, 24 September. https://www.tsf.pt/portugal/politica/jeronimo-acusa-costa-de-enfeitar-se-com -medidas-da-cdu-a-que-se-opos-11335800.html.

Twight, C. (1991) 'From claiming credit to avoiding blame: the evolution of congressional strategy for asbestos management', *Journal of Public Policy*, vol. 11, no. 2, pp. 153–186.

van Ditmars, M., Maggini, N. & van Spanje, J. (2020) 'Small winners and big losers: strategic party behaviour in the 2017 Dutch general election', *West European Politics*, vol. 43, no. 3, pp. 543–564.

Wolinetz, S. B. (1988) 'Party system change: past, present and future', in *Parties and Party Systems in Liberal Democracies*, ed S. B. Wolinetz, Routledge, London, pp. 296–320.

Demand without Supply? Populist Attitudes and Voting Behaviour in Post-Bailout Portugal

José Santana-Pereira ⓘD and João Cancela ⓘD

ABSTRACT

Unlike other European nations, Portugal has experienced an absence of relevant populist parties, even if its recent background of severe economic crisis could have been a fertile ground for their advent. To illuminate this apparent contradiction, we look at the demand side of the equation, drawing on survey data to examine the spread, correlates, and potential electoral implications of populist attitudes in Portugal. We show that while individuals with a populist outlook do not share a particular socioeconomic profile, several attitudinal factors are significant predictors of individual-level populism. Furthermore, those with stronger populist attitudes are not more likely to abstain in elections, but rather tend to vote for parties that exhibit some degree of populism in their rhetoric.

Reacting to the real-world events of the last decades, namely the *populist zeitgeist* (Mudde 2004), the electoral growth of populist parties in Europe and their participation in governments in several countries, political scientists have devoted a great deal of attention to the phenomenon of populism in Western democracies. Within this frame of research, Portugal has often been depicted as an exception, since no clear-cut populist party, either left- or right-wing, has developed within its party system, not even after the shockwaves created by the Great Recession and the 2011–2014 bailout (Lisi & Borghetto 2018; Lisi, Llamazares & Tsakatika 2019). Indeed, while the conditions to activate populist attitudes (Lisi, Llamazares & Tsakatika 2019; Hawkins, Kaltwasser & Andreadis 2020) and foster the success of populist forces – deep economic crisis, high perceptions of corruption, and lack of responsiveness (Lisi, Llamazares & Tsakatika 2019; Hawkins,Kaltwasser & Andreadis 2020) – caused populist actors to flourish in Spain, Greece, and Italy (cases in which these parties not only became relevant players but also entered the government), the same has not happened in Portugal.

The period since Portugal exited its bailout in 2014 has undoubtedly been marked by an innovative (and initially, by no means uncontroversial) government solution dubbed the 'contraption' (*geringonça*) – a minority Socialist government formally supported by the left-wing parliamentary parties. During this period, Portugal's status regarding populism suffered no change. In fact, within the European continent, only Malta shared Portugal's lack of relevant, unambiguously populist players (Rooduijn et al. 2019).

It has been argued that despite this contrast with most European countries (and especially with other Southern European polities), there have been important variations within the Portuguese party system in terms of the presence and salience of populist rhetoric across parties and over time (Lisi & Borghetto 2018). Comparative scholarship has also made the case that populism is a matter of degree rather than kind (Rooduijn & Pauwels 2011; Rooduijn & Akkerman 2017; Louwerse & Otjes 2019). However, even taking this into account, the Portuguese case is indeed remarkably distinct from other South European countries, as we show below.

Against this backdrop that allows us to depict Portugal as a (relatively) negative case of populism within Europe, several relevant empirical questions arise. First, to what extent is the lack of successful clear-cut populist parties in Portugal a match or mismatch with the demand side of the equation, namely citizens' general levels of populist attitudes? Second, assuming there is variation in terms of expression of populist attitudes, what are their underlying factors in Portugal, a context in which neither most parties nor the media (Caeiro 2019; Salgado 2019) have been keen to activate them? Finally, and perhaps more important, in the absence of straightforward populist choices in the electoral market, how do populist citizens vote? Do they abstain from voting or engage in forms of protest voting such as punishing the incumbent, supporting parties with some degree of populist substance, or voting in new players in the party system?

In this article, we draw on survey data collected between March and June 2018 (the beginning of the second half of the first-order electoral cycle) and in April-May 2019 (the eve of the European Parliament election) in order to examine the nature and correlates of citizens' populist attitudes in Portugal and the extent to which they are linked to different patterns of electoral behaviour: vote for parties according to their relative degrees of populism, for the incumbent, for new parties, and turnout. These data are not only recent but also one of the few sources of information about populist attitudes in the country.

The article is structured as follows. In the next section, we review the literature on populism and on this phenomenon in Portugal. Following that, we lay out the theoretical foundations of our study of populist attitudes, based on Mudde's 2004 definition of populism, and frame our expectations with reference to the results of previous research on the issue and the specific features of the Portuguese context. Then, we present the data and methodological approach chosen to test our hypotheses. The following section presents the results of the empirical analysis aimed at identifying the prevalence of populist attitudes in Portugal, their explanatory factors and correlates, and their impact on voting behaviour. The article concludes with a discussion of the main patterns identified.

Populism: the supply side and Portugal's exceptionalism in the South European context

In the last decades, the advent of populism has received a great deal of attention from scholars, pundits, journalists, and the general public interested in political affairs in Western democracies and beyond. Along with the growth of so-called populist parties in several countries (cf. Rooduijn et al. 2019), political scientists have increased their efforts to further understand the phenomenon.

However, at least from a conceptual and theoretical viewpoint, this field of research is remarkably fuzzy, with populism being defined as a political movement, style, discourse, strategy, culture, ideology, form of representation, or conception of democracy (Mudde & Kaltwasser 2017; Wuttke, Schimpf & Schoen 2020).

In spite of the conceptual richness of the field, a growing number of scholars are adopting the notion that populism constitutes a set of loosely articulated ideas which provide an interpretative framework of the political realm (Hawkins, Riding & Mudde 2012; Mudde & Kaltwasser 2017; Hawkins, Kaltwasser & Andreadis 2020). This ideational approach is best captured by Cas Mudde's (2004) minimal definition of populism, which is one of the most commonly used in empirical studies of this phenomenon. According to this author, populism is 'a thin-centred ideology that considers society to be ultimately separated into two homogenous and antagonistic camps, 'the pure people' versus 'the corrupt elite', and which argues that politics should be the expression of the *volonté générale* (general will) of the people' (Mudde 2004, p. 543).

As a thin-centred ideology, populism is able to combine with different leftist and rightist host ideologies (wider, deeper, and more substantive) such as socialism or nationalism (Mudde & Kaltwasser 2017; Rooduijn & Akkerman 2017). Some of the main components of this minimal definition (people-centrism, anti-elitism, and homogeneity of the people) were indeed identified by Rooduijn (2014) as the lowest common denominators observable in archetypical populist political actors across time and space.

Most of the extant literature has focused on the supply side of populism, i.e. political actors and, more concretely, political parties. Questions regarding the rise and success of populist parties, as well as their effects on the political system and the quality of democracy, have been thoroughly examined within the European context.[1]

Portugal's exceptionalism

As the salience of populism across Europe and interest in it have grown, Portugal has been often depicted as a case of absence of relevant populist actors. This is particularly noteworthy against the backdrop of political developments in other South European polities, in which populist actors have been quite successful (Lisi & Borghetto 2018; Lisi, Llamazares & Tsakatika 2019).

Granted, a few signs of populism are identifiable at the left-end of the Portuguese party system, in both the BE (Bloco de Esquerda – Left Bloc) and especially the PCP (Partido Comunista Português – Portuguese Communist Party), which has run in elections in a stable coalition with the greens since 1987. However, these signs are first and foremost rooted in these parties' main ideologies, which leads them to be sceptical of bourgeois/mainstream parties, European institutions, and financial/economic elites at large (Lisi & Borghetto 2018; Lisi, Llamazares & Tsakatika 2019). Indeed, Rooduijn et al. (2019) do not characterise these parties as populist, but merely as far-left and eurosceptic.

In turn, experiences of radical right-wing populism have been, largely speaking, unsuccessful – the far-right PNR (Partido Nacional Renovador – National Renewal Party) has never achieved more than 0.5 per cent of the popular vote and consequently has never entered parliament (Marchi 2013; Lisi, Llamazares & Tsakatika 2019). Other feeble populist parties and candidates have arisen in Portugal in the last decades but were unable to establish themselves as relevant players (Salgado & Zúquete 2017). It was only in October 2019 that a blatantly populist party, recently formed – Chega (Enough) – was able to secure one of the 230 seats in the Portuguese parliament (Marchi 2019; Mendes & Dennison 2020).

In order to better portray the presence of populist political parties in Portugal in comparative perspective, we rely on data from the 2017 Chapel Hill Expert Flash Survey (CHES; Polk et al. 2017). Specifically, we extracted the average expert classifications from two variables ('people vs elite' and 'antielite salience'). Both variables had values between 0 (not populist at all) and 10 (extremely populist). We used the classifications for each of the main Portuguese parties in these two variables and calculated their average, which produced a continuous variable, which we label anti-elite sentiment. The average of the values reached by each party weighted by the number of seats held in parliament yield 3.1 in the Portuguese case, which is moderately lower than in Spain (3.6), and considerably lower than in Italy (4.4) and Greece (5.7) for the same reference period.

Figure 1 plots the anti-elite sentiment scores of each party with seats in the national parliament on the vertical axis against the position of the party in terms of its overall ideological (left/right) stance on the horizontal axis.[2] These data

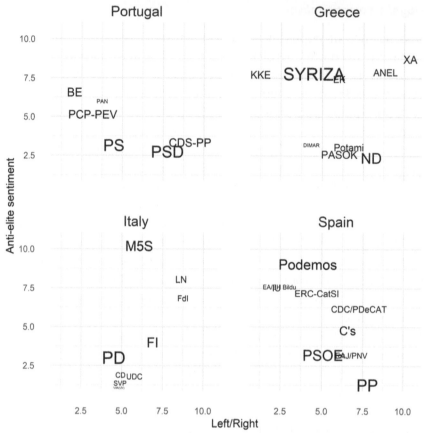

Figure 1. Distribution of South European parties along the left/right and anti-elite dimensions. Source: Own elaboration using data from the 2017 Chapel Hill Expert Flash Survey (Polk et al. 2017). Notes: For each figure, the horizontal axis represents the range of CHES scores in terms of Left/Right position (variable 'lrgen'), and the vertical axis represents the range of 'anti-elite sentiment', which corresponds to the average of the CHES variables 'people_vs_elite' and 'antielite_salience'. The size of each label is proportional to the number of seats in the legislature (as of 2017). Party acronym meanings– Portugal: BE (Bloco de Esquerda – Left Bloc), CDS-PP (CDS-Partido Popular – CDS-People's Party), PCP-PEV (also known as CDU; Coligação Democrática Unitária – Democratic Unitarian Coalition), PAN (Pessoas-Animais-Natureza – People-Animals-Nature), PS (Partido Socialista – Socialist Party), PSD (Partido Social Democrata – Social Democratic Party). Greece: ANEL (Anexartitoi Ellines – Independent Greeks), DIMAR (Dimokratiki Aristera – Democratic Left), EK (Enosi Kentroon – Union of Centrists), KKE (Kommounistikó Kómma Elládas – Communist Party of Greece), ND (Néa Dimokratía – New Democracy), PASOK (Panellinio Sosialistikó Kínima – Panhellenic Socialist Movement), Potami (To Potami – The River), SYRIZA (Synaspismó's Rizospastikís Aristerás – Coalition of the Radical Left), XA (Laïkós Sýndesmos: Chrysí Avgí – Popular Association: Golden Dawn). Italy: CD (Centro Democratico: Diritti e Libertà – Democratic Centre: Rights and Freedom), FdI (Fratelli d'Italia – Brothers of Italy), FI (Forza Italia – Forward Italy), LN (Lega Nord – Northern League), M5S (Movimento Cinque Stelle – Five Star Movement), PD (Partido Democratico – Democratic Party), SVP (Südtiroler Volkspartei – South Tyrolean People's Party), UDC (Unione di Centro – Union of the Centre), VdA (Vallée d'Aoste – Aosta Valley). Spain: C's (Ciudadanos: Partido de la Ciudadanía – Citizens: Party of the Citizenry), CC (Coalición Canaria – Canary's Coalition), CDC/PDeCAT (Convergència Democràtica de Catalunya/Partit Demòcrata Europeu Català – Democratic Convergence of Catalonia/Catalan European Democratic Party), EA/EH BILDU (Eusko Alkartasuna/Euskal Herria Bildu – Basque Solidarity/Unite Basque Country), EAJ/PNV (Euzko Alderdi Jeltzalea/Partido Nacionalista Vasco – Basque Nationalist Party), ERC-CatSI (Esquerra Republicana de Catalunya – Republican Left of Catalonia), IU (Izquierda Unida – United Left), Podemos (Podemos – We Can), PP (Partido Popular – People's Party), PSOE (Partido Socialista Obrero Español – Spanish Socialist Workers' Party).

show that levels of anti-elite sentiment were relatively lower in Portugal than in the other three countries, with the most populist party with parliamentary seats being BE (6.3 on a 0–10 scale), for the reasons explained above, followed by PAN (Pessoas-Animais-Natureza – People-Animals-Nature) (5.8). Much higher scores could be found in Spain, where Podemos (We Can) scored 8.7; in Italy, with the M5S (Movimente 5 Stelle – Five Star Movement) scoring 9.9; and in Greece, which featured high-scoring parties on both the radical left – SYRIZA (Συνασπισμός της Ριζοσπαστικής Αριστεράς – Coalition of the Radical Left) with 7.4, and the KKE (Κομμουνιστικό Κόμμα Ελλάδας – Communist Party of Greece) with 7.5 – and on the far right with XA (Χρυσή Αυγή – Golden Dawn) with 8.4.

Several factors have been put forward to explain the lack of success of populist parties in Portugal in the last decades, the majority of which have to do with the supply side. On the right end of the party system, there is the recent memory of the authoritarian Estado Novo regime (1933–1974), the lack of professionalism, strategy, and charismatic leadership of populist entrepreneurs, the absence of a refugee crisis, and the feeble salience of immigration as an issue are often mentioned factors. On the left, experts stress the fact that established radical left-wing parties have played a role in absorbing discontent and anti-austerity or anti-establishment social movements which in other South European countries led to the establishment of new populist parties, as well as their integration into the contract parliamentarism mode of government known as *geringonça* (contraption) between 2015 and 2019.[3] Less – or shall we say nothing? – is known about the demand side of populism in Portugal.

The demand side: populist attitudes, their correlates and implications

In spite of efforts aimed at identifying the social and attitudinal characteristics of populist party voters (e.g. Rooduijn 2018), researchers have been slow to adequately address the demand side of populism, namely by analysing the populist attitudes held by citizens, their correlates, and their impact on political behaviour. Indeed, most of the literature on populist attitudes is less than ten years old.

An important step in the development of this field of research was the methodological and empirical contribution by Akkerman, Mudde and Zaslove (2014). The authors followed the previous work of Hawkins, Riding and Mudde (2012) and surveyed Dutch citizens by presenting them with six statements aimed at measuring the elements present in Mudde's 2004 definition. Their results indicated that populist stances indeed constitute a distinctive and uni-dimensional political attitude.[4] Populist attitudes measured in this way consti-tute a separate dimension from other political attitudes such as elitism, pluralism, political trust, and external political efficacy (e.g. Akkerman, Mudde & Zaslove 2014; Geurkink et al. 2020). The scale designed by Akkerman, Mudde and Zaslove (2014) has been one of the most used in the literature on populist attitudes which we will review in detail in the following paragraphs.

One of the key goals in the literature on populist attitudes, beyond measuring their dimensionality and incidence within the population, has been the identification of factors explaining individual differences in their expression. These efforts have focused on an array of variables, such as age and gender (e.g. Hawkins, Riding & Mudde 2012; Elchardus & Spruyt 2016), socioeconomic status (income, occupation, and education; e.g. Elchardus & Spruyt 2016; Tsatsanis, Andreadis & Teperoglou 2018; Rico & Anduiza 2019), the media diet people follow (Hameleers, Bos & De Vreese 2017), general personality traits (Fatke 2019), or even conspiratorial mentality (Castanho Silva, Vegetti & Littvay 2017). Others have focused on correlates such as attitudes towards immigration and the European Union (e.g. Hawkins, Riding & Mudde 2012; Hameleers & De Vreese 2020), support for referenda (Jacobs, Akkerman & Zaslove 2018), ideological self-placement (e.g. Rico, Guinjoan & Anduiza 2017; Tsatsanis, Andreadis & Teperoglou 2018), or individuals' relationship with the sphere of politics (interest and partisanship; e.g. Hawkins, Riding & Mudde 2012; Müller et al. 2017). In the next paragraphs, the main hypotheses to be tested in the Portuguese context will be framed within the context of this growing bulk of research.

Hypotheses on the correlates of populist attitudes in Portugal

We start by hypothesising that citizens who we can describe as *losers of globalisation* (Kriesi et al. 2006), and are therefore more vulnerable to recent or potential economic and cultural changes in the society, will display higher levels of populist attitudes. A few studies have indeed observed a direct relationship between some or several socioeconomic variables and populist attitudes[5]; others have reported the mediating impact of other attitudes[6] or the role of emotions[7] in the process. Specifically, we expect higher degrees of populist attitudes amongst people whose work situation (*H1a*), social class (*H1b*), and education levels (*H1c*) may cause them to feel – or indeed be – more vulnerable in an economically open and mutable environment, especially in a context like that of Portugal in the aftermath of the deep economic and financial crisis caused by the Great Recession.

Second, populist attitudes will be more pronounced amongst those who hold more negative perceptions of the path followed by society – in short, a declinist worldview, according to Elchardus and Spruyt (2016). Inspired by this, we expect populism to be higher amongst those who negatively appraise the performance of the executive (*H2a*), the general situation of the national economy (*H2b*), and the proceedings of European Union institutions (*H2c*). Regarding the specific impact of government appraisal, our expectation is based not only on the aforementioned effects of declinist viewpoints but also on the fact that citizens who feel close to the incumbent party (or parties) tend to be less populist – if, of course, those parties are not populist themselves (Anduiza, Guinjoan & Rico, 2018; Rico & Anduiza 2019).

Our expectation regarding the impact of the assessment of the national economy is based on the findings of Anduiza, Guinjoan & Rico (2018) and Rico and Anduiza (2019), who show that sociotropic considerations are more powerful predictors of populist attitudes than egotropic perceptions or objective vulnerability. Moreover, a negative view of how things work in the EU may also be related to populist attitudes because euroscepticism is a key factor in countries as different as Greece and the Netherlands (Hameleers, Bos & De Vreese 2017; Tsatsanis, Andreadis & Teperoglou 2018; Hameleers & De Vreese 2020).

Third, we will test two contrasting hypotheses about the relationship between ideological self-placement and populist attitudes. On the one hand, some studies have shown that populist attitudes (measured after the ideational approach, i.e. lacking nativist and horizonal exclusionist accounts of who 'the people' are) tend to be higher amongst left-wing citizens.[8] On the other hand, a few studies have reported a positive relationship between ideological radicalism (being at the extremes of the ideological spectrum) and populist attitudes (Ivaldi, Zaslove & Akkerman 2017).[9]

In the case of Portugal, where an established left-wing or right-wing populist party is absent but where one can spot a few signs of populist discourse at the left end of the party system (Lisi & Borghetto 2018), testing the relative impacts of ideological self-placement and extremism on the display of populist attitudes is an interesting and enlightening endeavour. Our expectations are that either populist attitudes will be more common at the extreme left (*H3a*) or at both extremes (*H3b*) of the left-right continuum.

Fourth, we expect a correlation between interest in politics and party identification on the one hand and populist attitudes on the other. These expectations are based on the general assumption that in a context such as Portugal, in which populist political parties *strictu sensu* have been absent for a long time, closeness to the political sphere, whether it is informational or emotional, might reduce the odds of holding populist viewpoints. Specifically, drawing on the results of Müller et al. (2017) for the metropolitan regions of Paris and Zurich, we expect to find a negative relationship between interest in politics and populist attitudes (*H4a*). Also, we expect citizens who express a party identification to be less populist than those who do not feel close to a party (*H4b*).

Hypotheses on the relationship between populist attitudes and voting behaviour

In recent years, researchers have also investigated the extent to which populist attitudes explain political behaviour, namely the choices that people make at the polls. Several studies have found an impact of populist attitudes on support or vote for populist parties.[10] That said, the activation of populist attitudes seems to depend on political context: when comparing the cases of Greece and Chile, Hawkins, Kaltwasser and Andreadis (2020) observed that populist attitudes were widely disseminated in both countries, yet only in the former was support for populist parties – and the impact of populist attitudes on the vote – considerably high. The authors linked this with the general economic and political landscape: while Greece was dealing with a major economic crisis and corruption scandals, Chile ranked as one of the least corrupt countries in the world and was fairly stable in economic terms.

Interestingly enough, two studies by Van Hauwaert and Van Kessel (2018) and Loew and Faas (2019) showed that populist attitudes interact with economic policy preferences in the probability of voting for a left-wing populist party and, similarly, with cultural policy preferences in the odds of voting for a right-wing populist party: populist attitudes will only explain voting for populist parties if citizens do not hold clear-cut preferences that are congruent with the populist party's host ideology (anti-market or anti-open society). Populist attitudes thus work as a 'motivational substitute' for issue proximity and encourage support for populist parties whose positions on issues do not match our own (Van Hauwaert & Van Kessel 2018, p. 83).

But what can we expect in terms of the impact of populist parties in a context lacking overtly populist competitors such as Portugal? Four expectations will be tested. First, based on the ideas that populism is not a dichotomous phenomenon but a matter of degree (Rooduijn & Pauwels 2011; Rooduijn & Akkerman 2017; Louwerse & Otjes 2019) and that, despite the fact that no full-fledged populist parties existed during the time frame under analysis, there are differences in the degree of populism expressed by parties in Portugal (Lisi & Borghetto 2018), we expect populist attitudes to increase the odds of voting for the relatively more populist (or, shall we say, least un-populist) parties in the Portuguese party system (*H5*).

Second, based on the patterns identified by Anduiza, Guinjoan & Rico (2018) and Hameleers and De Vreese (2020), we expect that populist attitudes are negatively correlated with vote for the incumbent party (*H6*).

Third, Marcos-Marne, Plaza-Colodro and Freyburg (2020) showed that in Spain, populist attitudes increased the odds of voting for new parties, irrespective of how populist those parties were. In line with this, we expect that populist attitudes will be related to a higher likelihood of voting for new competitors in the Portuguese sphere (*H7*).

Our last expectation has to do with the relationship between populism and turnout, which is an underexplored debate in the literature. Previous research has shown that, in the Netherlands, non-voters rank high in terms of populist attitudes (Akkerman, Mudde & Zaslove 2014; Hameleers & De Vreese 2020), but an impact of these attitudes on the likelihood of turning out to vote has not been observed in Spain (Anduiza, Guinjoan & Rico 2018). In the case of Portugal, inspired by Costa Lobo (2019), we test the assumption that, in the absence of successful populist political entrepreneurship, a strategy of exit (abstention) is likely for citizens whose populist attitudes mean they feel dissatisfaction with the political offer or are anti-partyist (Bélanger 2004). We therefore expect that populist attitudes will increase the odds of not turning out to vote (*H8*).

Data and variables

We relied on survey data collected in 2018 and 2019 tapping populist attitudes and other variables relevant to empirically testing our hypotheses in routine and pre-electoral times. Two datasets were employed: the 2018 voter survey from the research project *Crisis, Political Representation and Democratic Renewal* (N = 1375), fielded between 26 March and 18 June (Freire, Lisi & Tsatsanis 2018) and the May 2019 *Sondagens ICS/ISCTE* poll (N = 802), whose fieldwork took place between 22 April and 3 May (Magalhães et al. 2019).

Populist attitudes were measured using the scale developed by Akkerman, Mudde and Zaslove (2014), composed of six items aimed at measuring the specific components of people-centrism, anti-elitism and popular sovereignty encompassed on the minimal definition of populism proposed by Mudde (2004). The items are presented in the Appendix 2, available online at https://doi.org/10.1080/13608746.2020.1864910. Comparative analyses of populist attitude scales have suggested that the instrument created by Akkerman, Mudde and Zaslove (2014) is one of the best available, since it ranks high in terms of internal consistency and external validity, is acceptable in terms of conceptual breath and cross-national validity (Castanho Silva et al. 2020), and is relatively resilient to different operationalisation strategies based on its three different core components (Wuttke, Schimpf & Schoen 2020).

We created a composite index of populist attitudes by taking the arithmetic mean of the answers to the six items (on a 5-point scale ranging from 1 – 'completely disagree' – to 5 completely agree'). The average levels of populist attitudes are rather high: 3.82 on the aforementioned scale (with a standard deviation of 0.63). Details about the distribution of the six items in the two surveys are reported in the online appendix's Table A.2 and Figure A1, but it should be stressed that responses to the six items were overwhelmingly tilted towards the 'populist' pole of the scale: the proportion of respondents disagreeing and strongly disagreeing does not go beyond 18 per cent for any of the questions in both surveys.

In order to further confirm the internal consistency of this index, we followed the approach of Hawkins, Kaltwasser and Andreadis (2020) and conducted a Mokken scale analysis. The results of the monotonicity checks validated our strategy, as all items obtained a score above the conventional 0.3 threshold. The three reliability measures (Molenaar Sijtsma statistic, Cronbach's alpha, and Guttman's lambda-2) all yielded scores above 0.75, which is further evidence of the adequacy of the arithmetic mean as a consistent indicator of populist attitudes.[11]

Hypotheses concerning the correlates of populist attitudes were tested by fitting two Ordinary Least Squares (OLS) regression models using the composite index outlined above as our dependent variable.

Testing *H1a* entailed using information on work situations collected in both surveys. Specifically, respondents classified themselves as pertaining to one of the following categories: employees (reference category), self-employed, retired plus housekeepers and informal caregivers, and unemployed. In order to test *H1b*, we relied on two distinct sources of information, depending on the survey at stake. The 2018 study included information on the respondents' economic backgrounds, and we created a dummy variable named *low social class*. A somewhat different procedure was followed for the 2019 study, as in that instance we only had information about the type of work performed by the respondents. In this case, manual labourers were coded as belonging to the *low social class* group. To test *H1c*, we use a dummy variable which is set to 1 if the respondent has ever enrolled in higher education and 0 otherwise.

Testing the three propositions under the label *H2* was made possible by using three variables pertaining to the respondents' evaluations of the economy over the previous year, their assessment of the executive, and their satisfaction with how democracy works in Europe. The three variables are ordinal, and higher values mean more positive views.

H3a, which related to the impact of ideological (left-right) position on the propensity to have populist attitudes, was accounted for by the self-placement of respondents on a classic 0–10 scale. The variable used for testing *H3b*, which posited that those farther away from the centre would be more likely to share populist attitudes, was extracted from the same variable: those at the central point of the scale (5) were labelled 'centrist', those in intermediate positions on either the left (3, 4) or right (6, 7) were labelled 'moderate', and the remaining respondents (0, 1, 2 on the left and 8, 9, 10 on the right) were labelled 'extremist'.

Lastly, the operationalisation of *H4a* (interest in politics) and *H4b* (party identification) was straightforward, as both surveys included questions about these two matters. The first independent variable is ordinal with higher values meaning a greater degree of interest, while the second is a dummy in which the value 1 means that the respondent feels close to a political party.

In addition to these variables, we also controlled for age and gender, since a few studies have shown that men tend to display more populist attitudes than women (Elchardus & Spruyt 2016; Spierings & Zaslove 2017; Fatke 2019) and that older citizens tend to be more populist than their younger counterparts (e.g. Müller et al. 2017; Rico, Guinjoan & Anduiza 2017; Tsatsanis, Andreadis & Teperoglou 2018). We also included a dummy for the survey year, although we did not expect differences between the two time points.

As to the hypotheses related to the impact of populist attitudes on voting behaviour (*H5–H8*), different models were computed, depending on the dependent variable to be explained. In order to test *H4*, which posited that those with more intense populist outlooks tend to vote for relatively populist parties, we took the values of the 2017 flash update of the CHES (Polk et al. 2017) described above. Specifically, we used the scores for each of the main Portuguese parties in the anti-elite sentiment dimension discussed earlier, which produced a continuous dependent variable.

The remaining hypotheses were tested via logistic regression models using specific dichotomies as dependent variables. The voting intention for the incumbent Socialist Party (PS, *Partido Socialista*) was operationalised using a dummy variable in which choosing the PS was coded as 1 and selecting another party was coded as 0. The same procedure was followed for measuring voting intentions for new parties, those that were founded in the five years previous to the survey and never elected members of parliament (coded as 1),[12] as opposed to all others (coded as 0). Finally, we tested the relationship between the populist attitudes index and the declared intention to abstain (1) versus the intention to vote (0).

While the models with the vote for mainstream parties ordered by their degree of populism and for the incumbents were computed for both 2018 (intention to vote in a hypothetical legislative election) and 2019 (intention to vote in the forthcoming EP election), the last two (vote for new parties and abstention) were only computed for 2019 due to lack of suitable data for 2018. All models were computed with a series of control variables aimed at ruling out effects of known factors of voting behaviour, both sociodemographic and attitudinal.

Results

The correlates of populist attitudes

The test of hypotheses 1–4 took the index of populist attitudes as a dependent variable and used a sequence of two models, the results of which are summarised in Table 1. The detailed statistical results are available in Table A.3 in the online appendix. In order to provide a more concrete understanding of the direction and magnitude of the findings, Figure 2 plots the predicted values of the dependent variable for different values of the independent variables

Table 1. Summary of results regarding the correlates of populist attitudes.

Hypothesis		Empirical results
H.1a	Higher degrees of populist attitudes are expected amongst people with a less stable work situation	✗
H.1b	Higher degrees of populist attitudes are expected amongst people from a lower social class	✗
H.1c	Higher degrees of populist attitudes are expected amongst people with lower education levels	✗
H.2a	Higher degrees of populist attitudes are expected amongst those who negatively appraise the performance of the executive	✓
H.2b	Higher degrees of populist attitudes are expected amongst those who negatively appraise the general situation of the national economy	✗
H.2c	Higher degrees of populist attitudes are expected amongst those who negatively appraise the performance of the proceedings of European Union institutions	✓
H.3a	Populist attitudes will be more common at the extreme left of the left-right continuum.	✗
H.3b	Populist attitudes will be more common at both extremes of the left-right continuum.	✓
H.4a	A negative relationship is expected between interest in politics and populist attitudes	✗*
H.4b	Citizens who express a party identification are expected to be less populist than those who do not feel close to a party	✓

Notes: ✗: not confirmed; ✓: confirmed; *: A small, significant effect in the opposite direction was detected.

according to the coefficients yielded by Model 2 (reported in Table A.3. in the online appendix).[13]

Our first set of hypotheses regarding the higher propensity of the *losers of globalisation* to display a populist outlook towards politics was not supported. Indeed, in neither of the two models did individuals dubbed as such seem particularly prone to sharing a populist worldview. Neither those with feebler work situations nor those from low social class backgrounds or with fewer years of education were more likely to espouse such views. This suggests that, by and large, the roots of populist attitudes in Portugal do not lie in personal economic grievances, which leads us to reject *H1* as a whole.

Conversely, two of the propositions regarding *status quo* assessments were met: those who evaluated the executive more positively (*H2a*) and those who were more satisfied with the way democracy works in the European Union (*H2c*) were less likely to espouse a populist stance towards politics. On the other hand, evaluations of the economy (*H2b*) were not related to populist attitudes – a finding that does not replicate the patterns identified by Anduiza, Guinjoan and Rico (2018) and Rico and Anduiza (2019). This set of results allows us to conclude that it may not be a declinist view of the world, but instead a negative appraisal of specific institutions, that is correlated with populist attitudes.

The relationship between ideology and our dependent variable also partially met our theoretical expectations. Populism did not seem more disseminated on one particular side of the ideological spectrum – neither left nor right – which leads us to reject *H3a*. Its prevalence was nevertheless more widespread among those closer to the extremes *vis-à-vis* centrists – a pattern also observed in France and the metropolitan region of Berlin (Ivaldi, Zaslove & Akkerman 2017; Müller et al. 2017). Thus, *H3b* is confirmed: more intense populist attitudes

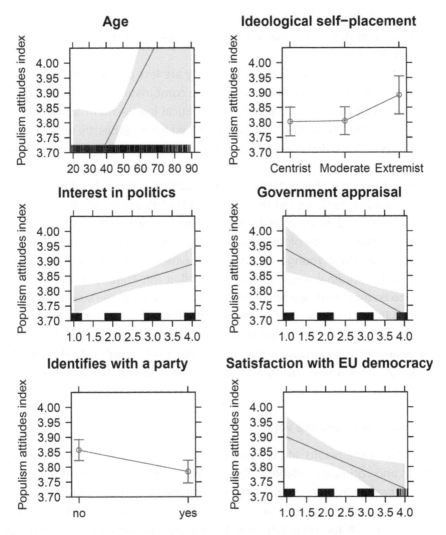

Figure 2. Factors impacting on populist attitudes in Portugal (2018–2019).
Source: Own elaboration using results from models reported in the online appendix.
Note: Figures plot the predicted values of the populism attitudes index for different values in
the independent variables according to the coefficients of model 2 (reported in table A.3 in the
online appendix).

are more abundant near both extremes of the axis, rather than in a specific
ideological bloc.

The two propositions laid out in *H4* yielded substantive results, albeit in one
of the cases in an opposite direction to what was initially posed. Indeed,
interest in politics was positively correlated with our composite index of
populism. This finding contradicts our initial expectation, insofar as in other
studies either the reverse was shown to be the case (in the metropolitan areas
of Paris and Zurich) or no effect was observed (metropolitan regions of
London and Berlin) (Müller et al. 2017). While we must acknowledge that the
effect is very small and barely statistically significant, this may mean that the

expression of populist attitudes in Portugal could be less about uttering stereotypes about a realm that people are dettached from, and more about critical citizenship.

By contrast, those who identify with a party are less populist in the attitudes they express towards the political system. The combination of these two results outlines a nuanced relationship between political involvement and populism: while it is true that those who are more detached from parties are more likely to adhere to populist beliefs, this group is not necessarily uninterested in politics writ large.

A last note on the effects of the control variables is due (cf. Table A.3 in the online appendix). First, we did not observe a statistically significant difference between men and women in terms of populist attitudes. Second, age is a significant factor, since older respondents tended to report higher levels of populism than their younger counterparts when several other sociodemo-graphic and attitudinal variables were controlled for. Third, populist attitudes seemed to be more widespread in 2019 than in 2018. While we lack a theoretical ground to frame this unexpected result, we believe that the different contexts (the 2018 survey was conducted in routine times and the 2019 survey in the midst of an election campaign) may help explain this result, with the populist attitudes of some citizens being activated by the electoral race dynamics.

Populist attitudes and the vote

A summary of the results of our analysis of the relationship between populist attitudes and voting is available in Table 2. We started by looking at the extent to which those with more intense populist attitudes were more likely to vote for parties that exhibit a relative degree of populist rhetoric (*H5*). This required examining the relationship between parties and populism as operating on a continuum, rather than in a dichotomous fashion. We estimated the relation-ship between the populist attitudes index and the degree of populism of the

Table 2. Summary of results regarding the relationship between populist attitudes and the vote.

Hypothesis	Empirical results
H5 Populist attitudes are expected to increase the odds of voting for the comparatively more populist parties	~ *
H6 Populist attitudes are expected to be negatively correlated with vote for the incumbent party	~
H7 Populist attitudes are expected to be related to a higher likelihood of voting for new competitors	✗
H8 Populist attitudes are expected to increase the odds of not turning out to vote.	✗

Notes: ✗: not confirmed; ~: partially confirmed; ✓: confirmed; *: The hypothesis was only confirmed in terms of voting intention for general elections, not in elections to the European Parliament party for which respondents intended to vote, both in hypothetical forthcoming general elections (2018) and in the European Parliament elections (2019).

The results show that the relationship is positive and statistically significant in the case of the former (column 1 of Table A.4 in the online appendix) but not in the latter (column 2 of Table A.4 in the online appendix). In other words, it seems that populist attitudes are a key factor in voting for relatively populist parties in Portugal only in hypothetical first-order elections, in which more is at stake and abstention or vote for fringe parties may feel like less legitimate vessels for such populist stances.

Regarding the controls, we see that ideology is significant in both elections, as the more left-wing respondents are, the more likely they are to vote for the more populist (or least non-populist) parliamentary parties in Portugal. This makes particular sense, since the highest degree of populism is found on the left side of the party system (Polk et al. 2017; Lisi & Borghetto 2018). In 2019, there was also an effect of radicalism, with respondents voting more populist the more they distanced themselves from the midpoint of the left-right spectrum. In 2019, age was also a significant predictor, reducing the odds of voting for parties with relatively higher levels of populism, but the size of this effect is modest.

The following hypothesis (H6) posited that respondents who scored high on the index of populist attitudes would be less likely to vote for the incumbent. The analysis of data from 2018 (Table A.5, in the online appendix, column 1) confirmed just that: the populist attitudes index was a strong negative predictor of votes for the incumbent Socialists, exerting an effect that was practically symmetrical to that of the popularity of PS leader and Prime Minister António Costa. Assessment of the state of the economy and ideological radicalism displayed the expected positive and negative impacts of voting for the party in office. However, an analysis of 2019 data (Table A.5, in the online appendix, column 2) did not replicate the negative impact of populist attitudes. Indeed, when asked who they would vote for in the forthcoming European Parliament elections, those with a more populist outlook did not exhibit a lower likelihood of voting for the incumbent. In terms of other results vis-à-vis the 2018 survey, it is also worth mentioning that self-employed and unemployed individuals, as well as those with higher levels of education, were less likely to vote for the PS.

Moreover, the populist index is not a very effective indicator of voting for new parties (Table A.5, in the online appendix, column 3), causing us to reject H7. In fact, regarding this dependent variable, only a few controls were significant – the odds of opting for them were higher amongst both the centrists and the ideologically extreme, than among those respondents who described themselves as moderately left-wing or moderately right-wing. Another finding was that the more positive the assessment of the government's record, the lower the probability of through voting for new parties. Lastly, it seems that self-employed respondents were more risk-adverse than those who worked for others, since their odds of supporting new parties was lower.

Our final hypothesis, *H8*, suggested that individuals with higher scores on the populist attitudes index would be more likely to abstain from voting in elections. However, this does not seem to be the case: such individuals were not significantly less likely to report an intention to turn out to vote in the next European Parliament election. This is shown in Table A.6 (in the online appendix), which contains two models. The first model is more parsimonious and features only sociodemographic variables, while the second is more complete and also encompasses attitudes and predispositions towards politics. Both models converge in signalling that Portuguese citizens espousing a more populist outlook are not especially detached from the electoral realm in comparison with other individuals.

An important caveat to take into account is that individuals were asked about their propensity to vote in a second-order electoral contest, and thus we should be cautious not to extrapolate this finding to other realms. Furthermore, in line with previous research (Smets & van Ham 2013), those who identified with a party were less likely to abstain from voting, as were those with a higher degree of interest in politics. Interestingly, contrary to trends detected in a recent analysis of general election data (Cancela & Magalhães 2020), it also seems to be the case that women are slightly more likely to participate than men.

In order to provide a clearer picture of these findings, Figure 3 presents four plots that convert the regression coefficients into expected values of each dependent variable. Since H5 is tested through a linear OLS regression, the interpretation is straightforward. When it comes to the testing of H6, H7 and H8, since the outcomes are both binary (voting/not voting in the PS, in new parties, and abstaining/not abstaining), the coefficients of the logistic regression were used to generate predicted probabilities. Figure 3 thus helps to make the case that there was a significant relationship between populist attitudes and party preference in the 2018 survey, but not with the likelihood of voting in a new party or turning out to vote (in this case, using the 2019 survey).

Taken as a whole, the results of the empirical tests for hypotheses *H5-H8* seem to indicate a higher likelihood of individuals with a higher propensity towards populist attitudes to find electoral options within the established party system – voting for relatively more populist parties – rather than looking for new parties or simply abstaining.

Conclusions

In this article, we reported the results of the first empirical analysis of populist attitudes in Portugal, a country which has been described as a negative case of the populist surge (e.g. Carreira da Silva & Salgado 2018) due to the

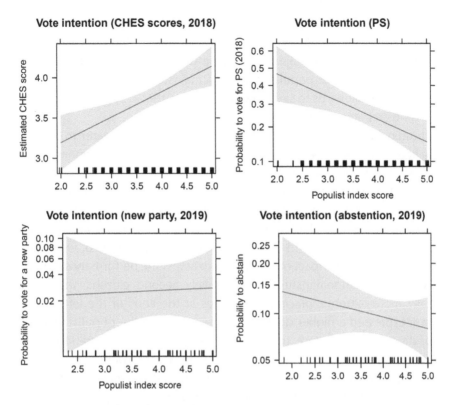

Figure 3. The impact of populist attitudes on voting intentions.
Source: Own elaboration using results from models reported in the online appendix.
Note: This figure plots the relationship between the values of the populist attitudes index and four dependent variables: degree of anti-elite score of preferred party (top left), using data from the 2018 survey; probability to vote in the PS (top right), using data from the 2018 survey; likelihood to vote in a new party (see text) in the elections to the European Parliament (bottom left), using data from the 2019 survey; likelihood to abstain in the elections to the European Parliament (bottom right), using data from the 2019 survey.

longstanding absence of clear-cut populist parties – either left- or right-wing – in parliament. Our results show that, in the post-bailout period, populist attitudes were considerably widespread in Portugal, confirming the assumption that the absence of relevant populist parties in the country has not been due to lack of demand, but is instead due to lack of supply – namely sophisticated and charismatic political actors able to choose the right substantive issues in order to thrive in a remarkably stable and closed party system such as that of Portugal.

The expression of populist attitudes seems not to be related to the specific socioeconomic position that individuals occupy in Portuguese society, as the losers of globalisation thesis (Kriesi et al. 2006) would suggest. In fact, the degree of agreement with the ideas of people-centrism, anti-elitism and homogeneity of both groups – highlighted in Mudde's (2004) influential definition and subsumed in the index we used in the empirical analysis reported here – is relatively the same for men and women; for people belonging to lower and

higher social strata; for the poorly and the highly educated; and for the unemployed, retirees, self-employed, and employees. This finding resonates with the
pattern identified by Rooduijn (2018) in his study of a different but correlated
phenomenon – vote for populist parties vs. mainstream parties in 15 European
countries – and allows us to say, paraphrasing him, that in socioeconomic terms,
there is no archetypal populist citizen in Portugal.

Attitudinal correlates of populist attitudes are, instead, clearer to spot. First,
those had a more negative evaluation of the government's performance and the
way democracy works in the European Union displayed higher levels of populist
attitudes. As mentioned above, unlike the appraisal of the government and the
EU, the assessment of the national economy was not a significant correlate of
populist attitudes and does not allow us to further corroborate the role of
a declinist view of the world (Elchardus & Spruyt 2016). Indeed, we might be
simply observing the impact of a tendency to assess the performance of political
elites and supranational institutions negatively. Second, citizens who are ideologically more extreme, placing themselves at the ends of the left-right continuum, expressed a higher degree of agreement with the populist worldview.
Third, those who feel close to a political party in Portugal were less likely to
embrace populist attitudes than those without a party identification – which
makes absolute sense in a context in which no blatant, salient populist creed has
been adopted by any relevant political competitor.

All in all, in attitudinal terms, strongly populist citizens are ideologically
radical, unhappy with the performance of political institutions, and unable to
find a party that they could care about. But they are not necessarily less
engaged or interested in politics, as we found the exact opposite relationship
between interest and populist attitudes. This would probably make it easier for
a new political force to activate these citizens' attitudes, granted that it could
distance itself from the disadvantageous epithet 'elite', since there is no need to
fight against the barrier of disinterest.

Also, do populist attitudes impact voting behaviour when there is no clear-
cut populist party to vote for? Our findings suggest that the answer is yes.
Although in Portugal citizens with higher levels of populist attitudes are not
more (or less) likely to support newer parties nor to abstain, they tend to
support parties that score higher on the populist rhetoric scale and are less
likely to vote for the incumbent party. This shows that in the absence of
a populist option in the political market, populist citizens may be drawn to go
for the second-best option, voting for moderately anti-elite parties and denying
electoral support to the governing party.

In the October 2019 legislative election, the new party Chega, a blend of
populism without a strong preference for direct democracy, on the one hand,
and a strong commitment to nationalistic ideals, on the other (Marchi 2019), was
able to elect one MP with 1.3 per cent of the votes, due to the concentration of its
electoral appeal in the country's largest electoral district, Lisbon (Mendes &

Dennison 2020). It is too soon to know whether its leader, André Ventura, will be able to succeed where others have failed and establish his party as a long-term relevant populist political force in Portugal or whether Chega is a short-time fringe phenomenon that will fade away as others have (cf. Salgado & Zúquete 2017). If the party grows exponentially from its current 1.3 per cent of the vote and one out of 230 parliamentary seats, we will be able to revisit the hypotheses tested in this article in a remarkably different context – one that would no longer allow us to describe Portugal as a negative case of populism in the European landscape.

Notes

1. For instance: Mudde 2013; Huber & Schimpf 2016; Mudde & Kaltwasser 2017; Rooduijn & Akkerman 2017.
2. The online appendix contains the scores of the variables for each party, as well as information about the sources of the data and the selected variables. This can be found in Appendix 1 and Table A.1.
3. Marchi 2013; Salgado & Zúquete 2017; Carreira da Silva & Salgado 2018; Costa Lobo 2019; Salgado 2019. For details on the geringonça: De Giorgi & Santana-Pereira 2016; Fernandes, Magalhães & Santana-Pereira 2018.
4. Interestingly enough, the actual uni- or multidimensionality of populist attitudes is an open debate in the literature, with studies supporting the idea that populist attitudes form a single construct (Akkerman, Mudde & Zaslove 2014; Boscán, Llamazares & Wiesehomeier 2018; Hameleers & De Vreese 2020; Geurkink et al. 2020) and others suggesting a multidimensional structure (e.g. Castanho Silva, Vegetti & Littvay 2017).
5. Hawkins, Riding & Mudde 2012; Elchardus & Spruyt 2016; Rico, Guinjoan & Anduiza 2017; Hameleers, Bos & De Vreese 2017; Müller et al. 2017; Boscán, Llamazares & Wiesehomeier 2018; Tsatsanis, Andreadis & Teperoglou 2018; Fatke 2019; Rico & Anduiza 2019.
6. For instance, in 2016 Elchardus & Spruyt observed that personal economic vulnerability translates into populist attitudes via increased feelings of relative deprivation and/or a declinist view of society (see also Rico & Anduiza 2019).
7. For example, anger resulting from the economic crisis in Spain resulted in higher levels of populist attitudes (Rico, Guinjoan & Anduiza 2017).
8. Rico, Guinjoan & Anduiza 2017; Tsatsanis, Andreadis & Teperoglou 2018; Rico & Anduiza 2019; but see Hameleers & De Vreese 2018 for an exception.
9. The same is reported in Müller et al. (2017) although only for the German sample.
10. Akkerman, Mudde & Zaslove 2014; Ivaldi, Zaslove & Akkerman 2017; Rico, Guinjoan & Anduiza 2017; Spierings & Zaslove 2017; Anduiza, Guinjoan & Rico 2018; Boscán, Llamazares & Wiesehomeier 2018; Hameleers & De Vreese 2018; Van Hauwaert & Van Kessel 2018; Geurkink et al. 2020.
11. Details about the distribution of the six items in the two surveys are reported in the online appendix's Table A2.
12. These parties are L (Livre – Free), NC (Nós Cidadãos – We, Citizens), A (Aliança – Alliance), IL (Iniciativa Liberal – Liberal Initiative), PURP (Partido Unido dos Reformados e Pensionistas – United Party of Retirees and Pensioners), and the pre-election coalition Basta, led by Chega's leader André Ventura.

13. Model 1 was fitted using only sociodemographic variables; in turn, Model 2 included the full set of variables after the addition of evaluative and attitudinal measures.

Disclosure statement

No potential conflict of interest was reported by the author.

ORCID

José Santana-Pereira ⓘ http://orcid.org/0000-0002-1713-3710
João Cancela ⓘ http://orcid.org/0000-0002-5055-2060

References

Akkerman, A., Mudde, C. & Zaslove, A. (2014). 'How populist are the people? Measuring populist attitudes in voters', *Comparative Political Studies*, vol. 47, no. 9, pp. 1324–1353. doi:10.1177/0010414013512600

Anduiza, E., Guinjoan, M. & Rico, G. (2018). 'Economic crisis, populist attitudes, and the birth of Podemos in Spain', in *Citizens and the Crisis: Experiences, Perceptions, and Responses to the Great Recession in Europe*, eds M. Giugni & M. T. Grasso, Palgrave, London, pp. 61–81.

Bélanger, E. (2004). 'Antipartyism and third-party vote choice: a comparison of Canada, Britain, and Australia', *Comparative Political Studies*, vol. 37, no. 9, pp. 1054–1078. doi:10.1177/0010414004268847

Boscán, G., Llamazares, I. & Wiesehomeier, N. (2018). 'Populist attitudes, policy preferences, and party systems in Spain, France, and Italy', *Revista Internacional de Sociología*, vol. 76, no. 4, pp. e110. doi:10.3989/ris.2018.76.4.18.001

Caeiro, M. D. F. (2019) 'Média e populismo: em busca das raízes da excepcionalidade do caso português', Master in Political Science Dissertation, ISCTE-Lisbon University Institute.

Cancela, J. & Magalhães, P. (2020). 'As bases sociais dos partidos portugueses', in *A Democracia Portuguesa 45 Anos Depois*, eds R. Branco & T. Fernandes, Assembleia da República, Lisbon, pp. 99–126.

Carreira da Silva, F. & Salgado, S. (2018). 'Why no populism in Portugal?', in *Changing Societies: Legacies and Challenges: Citizenship in Crisis*, eds M. Costa Lobo, F. Carreira da Silva & J. P. Zúquete, Imprensa de Ciências Sociais, Lisbon, pp. 249–268.

Castanho Silva, B., Jungkunz, S., Helbling, M. & Littvay, L. (2020). 'An empirical comparison of seven populist attitudes scales', *Political Research Quarterly*, vol. 73, no. 2, pp. 409–424. doi:10.1177/1065912919833176

Castanho Silva, B., Vegetti, F. & Littvay, L. (2017). 'The elite is up to something: exploring the relation between populism and belief in conspiracy theories', *Swiss Political Science Review*, vol. 23, no. 4, pp. 423–443. doi:10.1111/spsr.12270

Costa Lobo, M. (2019) 'Da ausência do populismo', *Expresso (Revista)*, 26 January.

De Giorgi, E. & Santana-Pereira, J. (2016). 'The 2015 Portuguese legislative election: widening the coalitional space and bringing the extreme left in', *South European Society & Politics*, vol. 21, no. 4, pp. 451–468. doi:10.1080/13608746.2016.1181862

Elchardus, M. & Spruyt, B. (2016). 'Populism, persistent republicanism and declinism: an empirical analysis of populism as a thin ideology', *Government and Opposition*, vol. 51, no. 1, pp. 111–133. doi:10.1017/gov.2014.27

Fatke, M. (2019). 'The personality of populists: how the big five traits relate to populist attitudes', *Personality and Individual Differences*, vol. 139, pp. 138–151. doi:10.1016/j.paid.2018.11.018

Fernandes, J. M., Magalhães, P. C. & Santana-Pereira, J. (2018). 'Portugal's leftist government: from sick man to poster boy?', *South European Society & Politics*, vol. 23, no. 4, pp. 503–524. doi:10.1080/13608746.2018.1525914

Freire, A., Lisi, M. & Tsatsanis, E. (2018), 'Portuguese citizens survey 2016–2018'. Dataset. Available online at: http://er.cies.iscte-iul.pt/

Geurkink, B., Zaslove, A., Sluiter, R. & Jacobs, K. (2020). 'Populist attitudes, political trust, and external political efficacy: old wine in new bottles?', *Political Studies*, vol. 68, no. 1, pp. 247–267. doi:10.1177/0032321719842768

Hameleers, M., Bos, L. & De Vreese, C. H. (2017). 'The appeal of media populism: the media preferences of citizens with populist attitudes', *Mass Communication and Society*, vol. 20, no. 4, pp. 481–504. doi:10.1080/15205436.2017.1291817

Hameleers, M. & De Vreese, C. H. (2020). 'To whom are "the people" opposed? Conceptualizing and measuring citizens' populist attitudes as a multidimensional construct', *Journal of Elections, Public Opinion and Parties*, vol. 30, no. 2, pp. 255–274. doi:10.1080/17457289.2018.1532434

Hawkins, K. A., Kaltwasser, C. R. & Andreadis, I. (2020). 'The activation of populist attitudes', *Government and Opposition*, vol. 55, no. 2, pp. 283–307. doi:10.1017/gov.2018.23

Hawkins, K. A., Riding, S. & Mudde, C. (2012). 'Measuring populist attitudes', Committee on Concepts and Methods Working Paper Series, University of Georgia.

Huber, R. A. & Schimpf, C. H. (2016). 'A drunken guest in Europe? The influence of populist radical right parties on democratic quality', *Zeitschrift fur Vergleichende Politikwissenschaft*, vol. 10, no. 2, pp. 103–129. doi:10.1007/s12286-016-0302-0

Ivaldi, G., Zaslove, A. & Akkerman, A. (2017). 'La France Populiste?' Working paper Available online at: https://hal.archives-ouvertes.fr/halshs-01491961/

Jacobs, K., Akkerman, A. & Zaslove, A. (2018). 'The voice of populist people? Referendum preferences, practices and populist attitudes', *Acta Politica*, vol. 53, no. 4, pp. 517–541. doi:10.1057/s41269-018-0105-1

Kriesi, H., Grande, E., Lachat, R., Dolezal, M., Bornschier, S. & Frey, T. (2006). 'Globalization and the transformation of the national political space: six European countries compared', *European Journal of Political Research*, vol. 45, no. 6, pp. 921–956. doi:10.1111/j.1475-6765.2006.00644.x

Lisi, M. & Borghetto, E. (2018). 'Populism, blame shifting and the crisis: discourse strategies in Portuguese political parties', *South European Society & Politics*, vol. 23, no. 4, pp. 405–427. doi:10.1080/13608746.2018.1558606

Lisi, M., Llamazares, I. & Tsakatika, M. (2019). 'Economic crisis and the variety of populist response: evidence from Greece, Portugal and Spain', *West European Politics*, vol. 42, no. 6, pp. 1284–1309. doi:10.1080/01402382.2019.1596695

Loew, N. & Faas, T. (2019). 'Between thin- and host-ideologies: how populist attitudes interact with policy preferences in shaping voting behaviour', *Representation*, vol. 55, no. 4, pp. 493–511. doi:10.1080/00344893.2019.1643772

Louwerse, T. & Otjes, S. (2019). 'How populists wage opposition: parliamentary opposition behaviour and populism in Netherlands', *Political Studies*, vol. 67, no. 2, pp. 479–495. doi:10.1177/0032321718774717

Magalhães, P., Ramos, A., Santana-Pereira, J., Costa Lobo, M., Pereira, M., Vicente, P. & Adão e Silva, P. (2019) 'Sondagem Maio 2019 para SIC/Expresso'. Available online at: https://sondagens-ics-ul.iscte-iul.pt/2019/05/17/sondagem-maio-2019-para-sic-expresso-parte-1/

Marchi, R. (2013). 'The extreme right in 21st century Portugal: the Partido Nacional Renovador', in *Right-Wing Extremism in Europe. Country Analyses, Counter-Strategies and Labour-Market Oriented Exit Strategies*, eds R. Melzer & S. Serafin, Friedrich-Ebert Stiftung, Berlin, pp. 133–155.

Marchi, R. (2019) 'Um olhar exploratório sobre o partido Chega', *Observador*, 21 December.

Marcos-Marne, H., Plaza-Colodro, C. & Freyburg, T. (2020). 'Who votes for new parties? Economic voting, political ideology and populist attitudes', *West European Politics*, vol. 43, no. 1, pp. 1–21. doi:10.1080/01402382.2019.1608752

Mendes, M. & Dennison, J. (2020). 'Explaining the emergence of the radical right in Spain and Portugal: salience, stigma and supply', *West European Politics*, pp. 1–24. doi:10.1080/01402382.2020.1777504

Mudde, C. (2004). 'The populist zeitgeist', *Government and Opposition*, vol. 39, no. 4, pp. 541–563. doi:10.1111/j.1477-7053.2004.00135.x

Mudde, C. (2013). 'Three decades of populist radical right parties in Western Europe: so what?', *European Journal of Political Research*, vol. 52, no. 1, pp. 1–19. doi:10.1111/j.1475-6765.2012.02065.x

Mudde, C. & Kaltwasser, C. R. (2017). *Populism: A Very Short Introduction*, Oxford University Press, Oxford.

Müller, P., Schemer, C., Wettstein, M., Schulz, A., Wirz, D. S., Engesser, S. & Wirth, W. (2017). 'The polarizing impact of news coverage on populist attitudes in the public: evidence from a panel study in four European democracies', *Journal of Communication*, vol. 67, no. 6, pp. 968–992. doi:10.1111/jcom.12337

Polk, J., Rovny, J., Bakker, R., Edwards, E., Hooghe, L., Jolly, S., Koedam, J., Kostelka, F., Marks, G., Shumacher, G., Steenbergen, M., Vachudova, M. & Zilovic, M. (2017). 'Explaining the salience of anti-elitism and reducing political corruption for political parties in Europe with the 2014 Chapel Hill Expert Survey data', *Research & Politics* 10.1177/2053168016686915

Rico, G. & Anduiza, E. (2019). 'Economic correlates of populist attitudes: an analysis of nine European countries in the aftermath of the great recession', *Acta Politica*, vol. 54, no. 3, pp. 371–397. doi:10.1057/s41269-017-0068-7

Rico, G., Guinjoan, M. & Anduiza, E. (2017). 'The emotional underpinnings of populism: how anger and fear affect populist attitudes', *Swiss Political Science Review*, vol. 23, no. 4, pp. 444–461. doi:10.1111/spsr.12261

Rooduijn, M. (2014). 'The nucleus of populism: in search of the lowest common denominator', *Government and Opposition*, vol. 4, no. 4, pp. 573–599. doi:10.1017/gov.2013.30

Rooduijn, M. (2018). 'What unites the voter bases of populist parties? Comparing the electorates of 15 populist parties', *European Political Science Review*, vol. 10, no. 3, pp. 351–368. doi:10.1017/S1755773917000145

Rooduijn, M. & Akkerman, T. (2017). 'Flank attacks: populism and left-right radicalism in Western Europe', *Party Politics*, vol. 23, no. 3, pp. 193–204. doi:10.1177/1354068815596514

Rooduijn, M. & Pauwels, T. (2011). 'Measuring populism: comparing two methods of content analysis', *West European Politics*, vol. 34, no. 6, pp. 1272–1283. doi:10.1080/01402382.2011.616665

Rooduijn, M., Van Kessel, S., Froio, C., Pirro, A., De Lange, S., Halikiopoulou, D., Lewis, P., Mudde, C. & Taggart, P. (2019) 'The PopuList: an overview of populist, far right, far left and Eurosceptic parties in Europe', available online at: http://www.popu-list.org

Salgado, S. (2019). 'Where's populism? Online media and the diffusion of populist discourses and styles in Portugal', *European Political Science*, vol. 18, no. 1, pp. 53–65. doi:10.1057/s41304-017-0137-4

Salgado, S. & Zúquete, J. P. (2017). 'Portugal: discreet populisms amid unfavourable contexts and stigmatization'. in *Populist Political Communication in Europe*, eds T. Aalberg, F. Esser, C. Reinemann, J. Strömbäck & C. De Vreese, Routledge, New York, pp. 235–248.

Smets, K. & van Ham, C. T. (2013). 'The embarrassment of riches? A meta-analysis of individual-level research on voter turnout', *Electoral Studies*, vol. 32, no. 2, pp. 344–359. doi:10.1016/j.electstud.2012.12.006

Spierings, N. & Zaslove, A. (2017). 'Gender, populist attitudes, and voting: explaining the gender gap in voting for populist radical right and populist radical left parties', *West European Politics*, vol. 40, no. 4, pp. 821–847. doi:10.1080/01402382.2017.1287448

Tsatsanis, E., Andreadis, I. & Teperoglou, E. (2018). 'Populism from below: socio-economic and ideological correlates of mass attitudes in Greece', *South European Society & Politics*, vol. 23, no. 4, pp. 429–450. doi:10.1080/13608746.2018.1510635

Van Hauwaert, S. M. & Van Kessel, S. (2018). 'Beyond protest and discontent: a cross-national cross-national analysis of the effect of populist attitudes and issue positions on populist party support', *European Journal of Political Research*, vol. 57, no. 1, pp. 68–92. doi:10.1111/1475-6765.12216

Wuttke, A., Schimpf, C. & Schoen, H. (2020). 'When the whole is greater than the sum of its parts: on the conceptualization and measurement of populist attitudes and other multidimensional constructs', *American Political Science Review*, vol. 114, no. 2, pp. 356–374. doi:10.1017/S0003055419000807

In the Shadow of the 'Government of the Left': The 2019 Legislative Elections in Portugal

Carlos Jalali (ID), João Moniz (ID) and Patrícia Silva (ID)

ABSTRACT

This article examines the Portuguese 2019 legislative election, which took place after a period of unprecedented and unexpected cooperation of the pro-European centre left and eurosceptic radical left. Initially dismissed as a 'contraption', this alliance belied the initial expectations and increasingly became a reference for South European social democratic parties. Yet, despite a seemingly reinforced popular mandate, it was not maintained after the 2019 election. We identify three factors for this. First, we suggest that the 2015–19 'contraption' was a case of weak contract parliamentarism, making it easier not to renew. Second, the electoral victory of the Socialist Party made deals between the left-wing parties less necessary. Third, enduring programmatic differences between those parties hindered cooperation. Finally, it should be noted that the 'contraption' impacted interparty relations on the left and the expansion in the number of parliamentary parties in 2019, notably on the right.

The 2019 legislative election came at a unique juncture in democratic Portugal. The post-bailout election of 2015 gave rise to a hitherto unparalleled governing arrangement, with a Socialist minority executive led by António Costa that was able to reach and remain in office thanks to parliamentary support from two radical left parties: the PCP (Partido Comunista Português – Portuguese Communist Party) and BE (Bloco de Esquerda – Left Bloc). Previously, neither had ever sustained a Socialist executive and the literature identified a significant ideological and historical chasm between the three parties. The exceptionality of this support was reflected in the popular designation that the arrangement received: the 'contraption' ('geringonça').

This designation initially sought to reflect its likely instability. The two radical left parties' deeply anti-capitalist (and, in the case of the Communist Party, Marxist-Leninist) stance, as well as their euroscepticism (particularly pronounced in the PCP), contrasted with the strongly pro-European and centre-left PS (Partido Socialista – Socialist Party). Moreover, while Portugal's bailout programme had formally ended in May 2014, the country continued to face considerable EU and market pressure to sustain fiscal consolidation.

The post-bailout Socialist government of António Costa thus seemed fated to fail, setting course between the Scylla of fiscal prudence and the Charybdis of reverting austerity that its radical left-wing partners demanded. Yet the Costa government successfully navigated this narrow strait. It was able to maintain the support of the PCP and BE while becoming an economic success story for EU bailouts. Its finance minister was elected President of the Eurogroup in 2017 and his German counterpart Wolfgang Schäuble dubbed him 'the Cristiano Ronaldo of Ecofin' (the Council of Economic and Finance Ministers of the EU). This made the 'contraption' also a rare success for the European left. As the Economist put it in 2018, there was a 'small miracle on the Atlantic', with the Costa government the exception to Europe's 'floundering social democracy' (Economist 2018).

The Portuguese 'contraption' quickly became a reference for many European social democratic parties. In a 2017 debate for the leadership of the Spanish Socialist Party (PSOE), the eventual winner Pedro Sánchez identified the 'Portuguese way' as a political solution for Spain (Público 2017), a position he would subsequently reaffirm. In the same year, the newly-elected winner of the French Socialist Party's presidential primary, Benoît Hamon, travelled to Lisbon to study the 'contraption', which he found to be a 'source of inspiration' (Bruckert 2017); and, a year later, the then-leader of Italy's Democratic Party, Maurizio Martina, praised the Portuguese 'experiment' as a model not only for Italy but for all of Europe (Sábado 2018). Indeed, the interest in Portugal's 'contraption' went well beyond Southern Europe (Valente 2017).

In this article, we examine the 2019 Portuguese legislative election and its bearing on the Portuguese party system. Yet we start the article with the 'contraption' because it was very much in the shadow of this domestically unprecedented and internationally alluring experiment that this election took place and its impact must be analysed. We thus explore how the 'contraption' influenced the 2019 elections in terms of the competing parties, their programmes and post-electoral government formation, dimensions that are of relevance not only to the Portuguese party system but potentially also to debates regarding cooperation between left-wing parties in Southern Europe, if not beyond.

This article begins by providing the context of the 2019 elections, particularly examining the nature of the arrangement between the three left-wing parties, before providing an overview of the main protagonists in these elections, including the more important new challenger parties that emerged. It then examines the electoral manifestos of the parliamentary parties, comparing their platforms in 2019 and 2015 before providing an overview of the election campaign. The final two sections examine the electoral results and the post-2019 government that emerged.

Context: the shadow of the contraption

The Portuguese parliament is elected by a closed-list D'Hondt PR system. Regarding government formation, the country's President designates a Prime Minister: by convention, the leader of the most-voted party following a legislative election. After this, a weak investiture regime prevails, with a negative majority in parliament required to reject the ensuing government (Cheibub, Martin & Rasch 2015). This facilitates the formation of minority governments. For an investiture to fail, a motion to reject the government's programme must be tabled by a parliamentary group and approved by 50 per cent+1 of all MPs in exercise of their office. Motions to reject have been largely symbolic in democratic Portugal.[1]

Yet this institutional element came to the fore in the 2015 legislative elections, giving rise to the 'contraption'. The two parties that governed during the 2011–2014 bailout period, the centre-right PSD (Partido Social Democrata – Social Democratic Party) and its junior coalition partner, the conservative CDS-PP (CDS-Partido Popular – CDS-Popular Party), contested these elections in a pre-electoral alliance, PAF (Portugal à Frente – Portugal Ahead). This joint list polled 38.6 per cent of the vote and surpassed the Socialists in terms of the popular vote by over six percentage points. While the PAF alliance was only electoral, with the two parties forming separate parliamentary groups, this result also granted the PSD the largest seat-share in parliament, with 89 seats in Portugal's 230-strong parliament, three more than the Socialists.

Convention granted the first opportunity to form a government to Pedro Passos Coelho, the leader of the PSD and prime minister from 2011 to 2015. However, his minority coalition government with the CDS-PP was rejected in a parliamentary investiture vote. The ensuing Socialist Party government headed by António Costa, that governed until the 2019 legislative elections, thus constituted the first instance of a government that did not emerge from the largest party parliamentary group or from the most voted list in the elections.

This unique outcome resulted from the Costa government obtaining unprecedented parliamentary support from PCP and BE. Not only did these two parties back the investiture of Costa's government, they also voted with the government on key policy instruments, most notably on the state budget. The exceptionality of this cannot be overstated. Previously, neither party had ever backed a budget presented by a Socialist executive – rather, in virtually every case, they had voted against.

This lack of cooperation on the left was seen as a central and defining characteristic of the country's party system (Jalali 2007), explained by both ideological and historical rifts. With regard to the former, the Socialist Party was a moderate, pro-European centrist social democratic party. In the 1990s, it warmly embraced 'Third Way' politics, abandoning the 'mostly rhetorical traditional Social Democratic components of its programme' (Lobo & Magalhães 2004, p. 84); and this positioning remained in its most recent period in office, from 2005 to 2011.

This stood in stark contrast with the Portuguese Communist Party, which remained, in the new millennium, an almost archetypical extreme-left conservative communist party, to use March's (2012, pp. 16–18) typology of radical left parties: Marxist-Leninist, largely endorsing the Soviet experience, with democratic centralism and strongly eurosceptic. As March (2012, p. 18) notes, these parties 'usually denounce all compromise with "bourgeois" political forces including social democracy', and that was certainly the case of the PCP, at least until 2015, in Portugal.

The position of the PS – and also of the PCP – equally diverged from that of the BE, which was initially founded in the late 1990s as an alliance of former Maoists, Trotskyites and disillusioned PCP dissidents. March (2012, pp. 16–19) places this party in the democratic socialist radical left type, which opposes both '"totalitarian" communism and "neo-liberal" social democracy'.

These ideological divisions were reinforced by historical ones. In Portugal's fraught revolutionary years of 1974–75, when the type of regime that would follow the authoritarian Estado Novo (1933–1974) was in the balance, the PS, PCP and the precursors of the BE were very much on opposite sides of the 'barricade' (Jalali 2007).

The run-up to the 2015 election did little to foreshadow their subsequent cooperation. The PCP remained firmly committed to its ideological stance, with former trade unionist Jerónimo de Sousa in his 11th year as party secretary-general. The BE also showed little programmatic divergence vis-à-vis earlier periods under the helm of Catarina Martins (one of two leaders during the brief bicephalous leadership of 2012–14, and sole leader since 2014). Finally, while the then newly-elected Socialist leader António Costa spoke of an overture to the parties to the Socialists' left (Pedroso 2014), his participation in the preceding 'Third Way' governments of the PS in the 1990s and 2000s suggested he was merely the latest Socialist leader paying lip service to cooperation on the left.

It was from these inauspicious beginnings that the 'contraption' was to emerge. Yet one of the unique aspects of this arrangement was that – consistent with the very notion of a contraption – its precise nature was never clear.

In popular and media parlance, the 'contraption' was largely seen as a virtual coalition between the three parties, evidenced for instance in Google Trends data.[2] This is consistent with Fernandes, Magalhães & Santana-Pereira's (2018) interpretation of it being an instance of Bale & Bergman's contract parliamentarism, i.e. the situation where the relationship between a formally minority government and the parties that support it in parliament is 'so institutionalized that they come close to being majority governments' (Bale & Bergman 2006, p. 422).

Yet revealingly, the three left-wing parties did not concur on the notion that the 'contraption' was 'close to being a majority government', and used the term in very differing ways. This is illustrated in the usage of the term 'contraption' in parliamentary debates over the duration of the Costa government from 2015 to 2019. The parties that most often used this term were the two right-wing opposition parties, the PSD and and the CDS-PP. Of the 'contraption' parties, the one that most used the expression was the PS, followed by the BE, with the PCP largely eschewing the term.[3]

This is also consistent with left-wing parties' and party leaders' descriptions of the government. Of the three, the Socialists emerge as the ones that most often used the term 'contraption'. A good example of this are the words of António Costa in early 2016, stating that 'they attempted to disparage' the government by 'calling it a contraption', but 'a contraption is an ingenious thing' and 'the majority demonstrates it is able to resist and is in good health' (Expresso 2016).

In stark contrast, we find the position of the PCP. This almost invariably described the 2015–2019 governing solution as a 'minority Socialist government' (Expresso 2019). Indeed, as the party's secretary-general remarked, this was the party's position from the outset, rejecting any model that could be understood as a 'government of the left, government of the lefts, government with parliamentary majority, government with parliamentary support' or even a 'parliamentary agreement' (Jerónimo de Sousa quoted in Serra Lopes 2019).

Between these two poles, though arguably closer to the Socialists' stance, we find the BE. Not only did the party mention the 'contraption' more often in parliament, the term was also more frequently used by its leading figures (see, for instance, examples in Expresso 2016). Yet this stance was not entirely consistent. While on some occasions the party leader Catarina Martins spoke of a 'minority Socialist government that was obliged to negotiate on the left' (Martins 2018), in others she described the post-2015 solution as a left-wing 'majority' (see Martins 2017).

Is, then, the 2015–2019 period an instance of contract parliamentarism? Public and media perception certainly match this characterisation of it being 'close to a majority government'. The same is true for the right-wing opposition parties, PSD and CDS-PP, at least in their parliamentary engagement with their left-wing counterparts. The latter, however, present a more nuanced perspective. If one were solely exposed to the PS's descriptions (and, albeit to a lesser extent, those of the BE), the notion of contract parliamentarism would seem to fit the bill. However, if one were to hear only the PCP's pronouncements, that would appear widely off the mark.

A more formal analysis of the Portuguese case between 2015–2019 suggests we may need to distinguish between *weak* and *strong* contract parliamentarism, extending Fernandes, Magalhães & Santana-Pereira's (2018) apt description of 'contract parliamentarism à la Portuguese'. The 2015 agreements between the left-wing parties meet the three criteria that Bale and Bergman (2006, p. 424) set out for contract parliamentarism: (1) the existence of a written contract that (2) is available publicly and (3) commits 'the partners beyond a specific deal or a temporary commitment'. In the case of Portugal, the PS signed documents with the PCP and the BE in November 2015, and the documents were made available to the public.

Yet the Portuguese case does introduce some variation to Bale & Bergman's original formulation. First, the agreement was not one of the three parties, but rather a combination of two bilateral agreements: one between the Socialists and the Communists; the other between the Socialists and the BE.[4] This contrasts with the instances of multiparty contract parliamentarism in Sweden noted by Bale and Bergman (2006, p. 433), where the three parties signed a single joint agreement. Likewise, PS, PCP and BE did not have joint meetings. Rather, the PS would meet separately with each party. Indeed, the PCP explicitly precluded any trilateral agreements or meetings, making that one of its 'red lines'. Jerónimo de Sousa explained that this was to avoid having a 'government sustained by a parliamentary agreement' rather than a 'minority government of the PS' (Jerónimo de Sousa in Serra Lopes 2019). However, this refusal also reflected the enduring ideological and historical divisions between PCP and BE.

Second, the bilateral agreements between the parties were actually quite weak. Not only were the agreements not dubbed as such – rather, they were titled 'Joint positions [of the parties] regarding the political solution' ('Posição conjunta do PS e do PCP sobre solução política' and 'Posição conjunta do Partido Socialista e do Bloco de Esquerda sobre solução política') – but they were also quite scant on substantive commitments beyond the formation of a Socialist government. Thus, if we take the PS-PCP and PS-BE joint positions, these list in section 3 a host of policy domains 'where it is possible to converge' and several outlined broad general objectives rather than specific policy measures, e.g. 'a decisive combatting of precarious working conditions' (PS & BE 2015, p. 1; PS & PCP 2015, p. 1).

In terms of political commitments, both documents stated that the parties agree to block a PSD/CDS-PP government; to enable the PS to form a government; and 'on the basis of the new institutional correlation in Parliament, to adopt measures that correspond to the aspirations and rights of the Portuguese people'. However, the documents fell short of even ensuring support for the government in confidence and supply votes. Rather, they merely set out that such votes (e.g. motions of no-confidence, legislation with budgetary impact, proposals from other parties and other important proposals) will be bilaterally examined (PS & BE 2015, p. 3; PS & PCP 2015, p. 2).

The Costa government of 2015–19 proved stable and resilient, as well documented in Fernandes, Magalhães and Santana-Pereira (2018). But this occurred with weak initial contracts between the parties. Adapting Bale & Bergman's (2006) formulation, these contracts generated 'minority governance'; but did so without necessarily 'being close to a majority government'. At the same time, the Portuguese experience does yield two potential implications. First, it suggests that it can be costly for parties to rescind even weak contracts during a legislature when the government enjoys favourable winds such as a recovering economy and a well-perceived performance. Second, it suggests the role of agency in minority governance contexts: the 2015–19 government might well have been less stable with other political figures leading negotiations within the parties.

In economic terms, the 2019 election took place under broadly favourable conditions. Average GDP growth stood at 2.4 per cent between 2015 and 2019, well above the two preceding legislatures (average of −1 per cent in 2009–11; −0.8 per cent in 2011–2015) (Eurostat 2020a). Unemployment practically halved, from 12.4 per cent in October 2015 to an average of 6.6 per cent from September 2018 to September 2019 (Eurostat 2020b). In both cases, Portugal outperformed the EU and eurozone averages from 2017–2018 onwards.

Policy-wise, the Costa government pursued its stated goal of 'turning the page on austerity' – the very first goal in the government's programme (XXI Governo Constitucional 2015, p. 4) – albeit at a gradual pace, simultaneously ensuring budgetary consolidation. These measures, including the reversal of previous cuts to pensions and public sector wages and the reduction of public transport prices in major cities, proved largely popular.

The country also saw its EU Excessive Deficit Procedure closed in 2017. The budget deficit averaged 1.9 per cent in the years 2015–2019, setting consecutive records in democratic Portugal with a deficit of 0.4 per cent in 2018 and a surplus of 0.2 per cent in 2019 (Eurostat 2020c). This compares with average deficits of 9.7 per cent during the 2009–2011 legislature and 5.8 per cent from 2011–2015.

Continuity and change in political parties and leaders

In terms of the protagonists in the 2019 elections, there was a marked difference between the parties on the left (PS, PCP and BE) and those on the right. The former retained the party leaders of 2015 and their party structures remained largely unchanged. There was also continuity in PAN (Pessoas-Animais-Natureza – People-Animals-Nature), a pro-animal rights and environmental party founded in 2011 that entered parliament in 2015, winning a seat for its leader, André Silva. PAN approached the 2019 election bolstered by the public subventions and greater media visibility that came with being in parliament, the former contributing to a more than fourfold increase in its campaign budget.

On the right, the scenario was of very significant turmoil, which went beyond the habitual internal factionalisation that accompanied periods of opposition, especially in the PSD (Jalali 2006). As the 'contraption' became more enduring, this reinforced ongoing debates regarding the future of the Portuguese right, which perceived the unprecedented cooperation between PS, PCP and BE as a seismic shift towards the left in terms of policy and the party system.

Despite its misleading name, the PSD is the largest party on the right and has alternated in power with the Socialists since 1976, usually with a centrist positioning (Jalali 2007). In the PSD, the 'contraption' reinforced the ongoing internal debate regarding its programmatic stance: whether it should position itself more on the right, in clear opposition to the 'contraption', or whether it should seek the centrist ground and cooperate with the PS. While the first strategy was pursued by Pedro Passos Coelho, the party's heavy defeat in the October 2017 local elections propelled his resignation as party leader.

He was replaced by Rui Rio, who defeated former prime minister Pedro Santana Lopes for the leadership in early 2018. Rio had been a critic of the austerity policies of Passos Coelho and adopted a centrist and conciliatory tone, pledging to collaborate with the Socialist government in key reforms. However, Rio's victory did not settle this internal debate. His strategy was deeply unpopular in parts of the party, which desired a more vehement opposition towards the 'contraption'. While Rio was able to quell the internal rebellions, these sapped his leadership.

To the right of the PSD is the CDS-PP, the frequent coalition partner of governments headed by the PSD. Historically it represents a more conservative electorate. It saw a leadership change in 2016, as its long-time leader Paulo Portas – who had first led the party in 1998 – chose not to run again. His replacement, the former Minister for Agriculture (2011–2015) Assunção Cristas, engaged in a more forthright opposition to the Costa government and the 'contraption', taking advantage of the internal travails within the PSD. Buoyed by her comparatively strong showing in the 2017 local election – in which she ran for Mayor of Lisbon and came second, beating the PSD's candidate – Cristas self-styled herself as the de facto leader of the opposition (Cunha & Matos 2019), ambitiously aiming to overtake the PSD as the largest party on the right (Correio da Manhã 2018).

While some on the right argued that PSD and CDS-PP should again contest the election in a joint list, as in 2015 (e.g. Mendes 2018), the two party leaders never seemed inclined to do so. In part, this reflected their immediate political strategies: a joint list precluded Cristas' attempt at a *sorpasso* on the right and went against Rio's centrist positioning for the PSD. It also reflected the two parties' differences. While PSD and CDS-PP always form coalition governments when their combined seat shares constitute a parliamentary majority, joint party lists at legislative level are few and far between (occurring only in 1979–80 and 2015).

The 'contraption' strengthened the perception that the party system was ripe for a reconfiguration, with a record number (21) of political parties running in the 2019 elections. This increase was particularly relevant on the right, with three new parties worth highlighting.

The first is A (Aliança – Alliance). Shortly after losing his bid for the PSD leadership, Pedro Santana Lopes formed this party, seeking to appeal to disaffected voters on the right. Having a former prime minister at the helm gave Aliança considerably more media attention than other non-parliamentary parties. Likewise, the party included a number of former PSD party bosses at local and regional level (e.g. Luís Cirilo, of Guimarães, *inter alia* former deputy secretary-general of the PSD), raising expectations that it could make significant electoral inroads.

A second notable party was CH (Chega – Enough), which emerged as the first radical right populist party in Portugal with prospects of entering parliament. Formalised in April 2019, Chega was very much the personal project of André Ventura. Previously a relatively unknown figure – best known for being the representative of Benfica in a cable football discussion programme and a columnist in a tabloid newspaper – Ventura shot to relative notoriety during the October 2017 local election campaign. As the PSD's mayoral candidate for the Lisbon suburb of Loures, Ventura made very charged comments that were not usual in the country's main parties and drew accusations of racism. He claimed, for example, that Portugal was 'too tolerant with some minorities', particularly the Roma people, and that 'gypsies live almost exclusively from State handouts' while failing to abide by the rule of law (Sol 2017). In September 2018, Ventura again gained some political prominence, when he began collecting signatures for an early PSD congress to remove Rui Rio from the party leadership (Diário de Notícias 2018). However, in early October, Ventura left the PSD, claiming he had been 'betrayed and stabbed in the back', and began forming his own party (Público 2018).

Chega can be seen as a populist party, following the definition of populism by Mudde and Kaltwasser (2017, p. 6) as a 'thin-centred ideology' that divides society into two opposing groups, 'the pure people' versus 'the corrupt elite' and views politics as 'an expression of the volonté générale of the people'. As Ventura put it in an interview with El País, 'we are an anti-system party', 'a party of the common people, not of elites, of people who suffer with the current system' (Del Barrio 2019). The party presented a strong emphasis on law and order issues (e.g. advocating in its programme the chemical castration of sexual aggressors, the introduction of life imprisonment) and nativism (e.g. decrying the 'globalist ideology', 'political correctness' and 'cultural Marxism'), consistent with the radical right populist type defined by Mudde and Kaltwasser (2017).[5]

The third noteworthy party on the right was IL (Iniciativa Liberal – Liberal Initiative). Founded in 2017, IL initially positioned itself as both socially and economically liberal, defending not only free market policies but also the curtailing of interference in personal affairs, e.g. defending adoption rights for same-sex couples and abortion (Oliveira 2017). However, in the run-up to the 2019 election, it was the party's economic stance that gained emphasis. Indeed, the party's 2019 manifesto was almost entirely focussed on reducing the role and size of the state, with virtually no reference to extending individual liberties.

This pivot is in part a reflection of the party's leadership change in October 2018. The new party leader was Carlos Guimarães Pinto, a young economics academic and consultant who came from the milieu of liberal political blogs.

It is worth noting that these three new challengers on the right can be largely traced to the 'contraption'. In the absence of this left-wing coopera- tion and the continuation of the Passos Coelho government after 2015, it seems highly unlikely that these parties would have emerged or gained salience. In the case of Aliança and Chega, it seems fairly certain that their founders would not have left the PSD if the latter was in government. As for IL, its laissez-faire economic programme would have been considerably undercut with the free market Passos Coelho in office. By pulling the ensuing government leftwards, the 'contraption' opened space for more opposition on the right.

Indeed, the effect of the 'contraption' is also perceptible in the one salient challenger on the left, L (Livre – Free), a left-libertarian pro-European party formed in 2014. While Livre did not win seats in the 2015 election, its key founding political platform – that the left-wing parties in Portugal should cooperate and converge – was largely vindicated in the subsequent 'contrap- tion'. The Livre campaign heavily featured its top candidate in the Lisbon constituency, Joacine Katar Moreira, making the 2019 election the first in which a black Portuguese became highly visible in the campaign.

Enduring positional and policy differences

In this section, we examine parties' programmatic positions relative to each other in the 2019 elections, and how these shifted compared to the 2015 election. This will allow us to, first, establish parties' relative positions in 2019; and, second, to gauge the impact of the 'contraption' on party platforms. Regarding the latter, we are particularly interested in assessing whether the cooperation of 2015–2019 heralded greater policy proximity on the left, an important dimension in terms of measuring the impact of the 'contraption' on the party system.

To estimate parties' positions, we apply unsupervised ideological scaling, the Wordfish algorithm, to their election manifestos (BE 2015; BE 2019; PCP 2015, 2019; PAF 2015; CDS-PP 2019; PSD 2019; PS 2015, 2019; PAN 2015, 2019), in order to estimate political positions from text. This technique analyses word frequencies of texts along a single-issue dimension (Slapin & Proksch 2008). Wordfish assumes that politicians and/or political parties' policy positions inscribed in text affects the rate at which certain words are used in the texts. Wordfish places each party/document in a scale that ranges from -2 to 2.[6] The algorithm provides a reliable and replicable form of analysis of great volumes of text in an easy fashion, forgoing the need for a team of human coders, thus providing researchers with the tools for the analysis of political texts. Following

Slapin and Proksch (2008, p. 709), we interpret the estimates from the documents as a whole as representing parties' positions on the 'left-right politics dimension'.

Likewise, we apply the technique to the parts of the manifestos that cover two specific topics: the economy; and European integration.[7] The first is a key policy area in Portuguese elections (Lobo & Pannico 2020), and all the more so in the post-bailout context. Regarding European integration, we want to assess to what extent positions changed since the post-bailout elections of 2015, which had followed a legislature in which the EU had loomed large over Portuguese politics. In contrast, in the post-post-bailout election of 2019, external (and notably European) constraints were less salient.

We should also clarify our treatment of the PSD and CDS-PP. As noted earlier, the two parties ran in an alliance, PAF, in 2015, before returning to their habitual separate lists in 2019. We thus compare the 2019 electoral manifestos of the two parties with their joint manifesto under the PAF alliance, thus seeing how they diverged away from their previous common position.

Let us begin by analysing the overall positions of the six parties that held seats in the 2015–2019 legislature, comparing their manifesto positions in the 2015 and 2019 elections (Figure 1). Four main conclusions emerge. First, there was a great degree of stability in parties' relative positions. Second, and related, the experience of the 'contraption' did not bring the parties on the left closer together. Rather, in 2019 the PS was closest to the PSD, just as in 2015 it had been closest to PAF. Meanwhile, the PCP and the BE remained in a quite distinct political space, with seemingly little effect of the 'contraption'. This result is not inconsistent with our interpretation of the 2015–2019 as a weak form of contract parliamentarism.

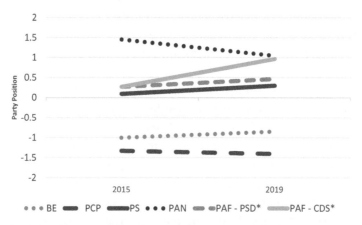

Figure 1. The left-right positioning of Portuguese parties in the 2015 and 2019 elections.
Source: Wordfish estimations from the analysis of parties' electoral manifestos.
Note: * In 2015, both the PSD and the CDS-PP start from the same position because these parties ran together in the PAF alliance.

Third, the post-PAF trajectories of CDS-PP and PSD revealed a considerable distancing of the erstwhile allies. The PSD presented a fairly centrist position, not distant from that of the PS, coherent with the attempts by Rio to occupy the centre-ground. As for the CDS-PP, it moved away from the PSD (and the joint PAF position), possibly reflecting the party's attempt to win over right-wing voters disenchanted with the PSD's centrism. Finally, we see a relative 'normalisation' of PAN, which had been a clear outlier in 2015. This is not surprising: the bulk of PAN's 2015 programme had centred on animal rights, something that found virtually no echo in other party platforms. In 2019, PAN became less of an outlier: a reflection of the pressures to be more than a single-issue party after entering parliament and gaining national visibility.

The parties' economic platforms (Figure 2a) also confirm that the 'contraption' did not generate programmatic rapprochement. Despite the four years of 'joint positions' on the left, the PS remained closest to the PSD on economic issues. Meanwhile, the PCP and the BE occupied a space of their own, quite

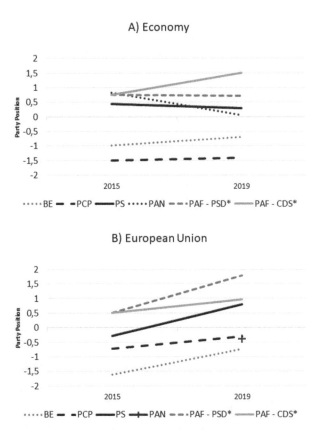

Figure 2. The positions of Portuguese parties in the elections of 2015 and 2019.
Source: Wordfish estimations from the analysis of parties' electoral manifestos.
Note: * In 2015, both the PSD and the CDS-PP start from the same position because these parties ran together in the PAF alliance.

distant from the other parties. Finally, here too PAN became less of an outlier, as its programme evolved beyond the single-issue focus of 2015.

Regarding European integration (Figure 2b), the evolution of the parliamentary parties' positions confirms a clear divide between the more pro-European PS, PSD and CDS-PP versus the more eurosceptic PCP and BE. PAN emerged closer to this latter group. More importantly, there does not appear to be a greater proximity on the left after the 'contraption'. Indeed, if anything, the distance between the Socialists and their radical left counterparts regarding European issues grew in 2019.

Looking at the text of the manifestos, there was a stark omission in the programmes of most parliamentary parties: references to the Costa government's left-wing parliamentary support. PAN and the PSD made no reference at all to this in their manifestos. Only the CDS-PP alluded to the 'contraption' (albeit avoiding the epithet itself), twice referencing the 'government of the lefts'.

More surprisingly, the picture was very similar among the 'contraption' parties themselves. The Socialist Party manifesto made no reference to the governing arrangement of 2015–19 or to its erstwhile partners, only talking of the 'government of the PS'. The same was largely true of the Communist Party. While it did have a brief section covering the previous legislature, it never mentioned the 'joint position' with the Socialist Party, rather choosing to reference the 'defeat' of the PSD/CDS-PP coalition. Likewise, the executive was described as the 'government of the PS' (PCP 2019, p. 62). The only partial exception was the BE, which covered the preceding legislature in a three-page section titled 'How we got here: 2015–2019'. Here, the BE mentioned the agreements of the PS with the left-wing parties and emphasised the gains achieved with these agreements, though it also decried the limitations of the 'government of the PS' (BE 2019, p. 31).

The election campaign

While the 'contraption' may not have featured in the manifestos, it was very much at the heart of the campaign. This was dominated by the question whether a 'contraption 2.0' would emerge after the elections and what government options would prevail.

The PS entered the key month of September with a commanding lead of some 20 percentage points over the PSD (Figure 3). Moreover, its poll result of 42 per cent in late August placed it within touching distance of a parliamentary majority, thanks to Portugal's less-than-proportional electoral system (for more on the electoral system, see Jalali 2007). The PS campaign emphasised its achievements in government, seeking to capitalise on strong economic performance, as well as on 'turning the page' on austerity while maintaining budgetary consolidation. The Socialist Party carefully avoided appealing for an outright parliamentary

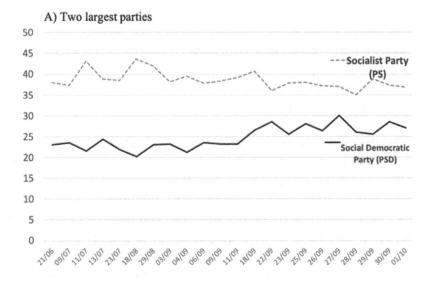

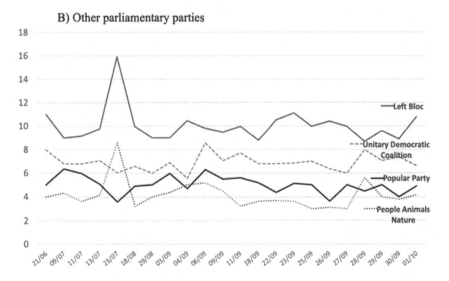

Figure 3. Trends in voting intentions during the 2019 Portuguese election campaign. Source: Authors' elaboration of data from Rádio Renascença's Poll of Polls (https://rr.sapo.pt/sondagens/).

majority during the campaign, though also not discouraging one. Instead, the Socialists called for a 'stronger Socialist Party' (Meireles, Guerreiro & Matos 2019). While not reneging on the 'contraption' – indeed, Costa stated that he would seek to make deals with PCP and BE even if his party won a parliamentary majority – it warned that a 'weak PS' would lead to instability (Cunha & Matos 2019; Meireles, Guerreiro & Matos 2019). In particular, Costa aimed crosshairs on the BE, arguing that a stronger BE would disrupt Portugal's stability, while sparing the PCP, in which he perceived a greater 'institutional maturity' (Dinis & Matos 2019).

Meanwhile, the remaining parties campaigned against the prospect of a PS majority, albeit following different logics. On the right, the PSD tried – despite the polls – to position itself as the alternative to the PS at the helm of government, while the CDS-PP tried to proclaim itself as the de facto leader of the opposition. On the left, the BE sought to take the credit for its role in the previous legislature, not least as opinion polls suggested that voters were sceptical of a PS majority and preferred the continuation of the 'contraption' (RTP 2019). The party's message was to claim the laurels for reducing austerity (viz. Catarina Martins claiming that 'everything that this political solution changed in the country' was due to the BE), while blaming the PS for expenditure freezes in public services to achieve budget deficit targets, asking voters to strengthen its hand so it could achieve even more (BE 2019, p. 31). As for the PCP, its overall message was not very different, declaring its achievements in protecting and restoring rights but also decrying that these did not go further because 'the PS did not allow it' (PCP 2019, p. 10). It also warned of a regression if the 'PS ends up with its hands free' (Eco 2019).

Where the two radical left parties diverged was on their stance regarding future deals with the Socialists if the PS won with a parliamentary plurality. The PCP rejected any possibility of another written document and stated that it would evaluate Socialist proposals on a case-by-case basis (Lopes 2019). The BE, on the other hand, kept its cards closer to its chest, claiming that the future solution would depend on citizens' votes (Henriques 2019). Meanwhile, with the polls putting the PS close to a majority and PAN near the 4 per cent mark, the possibility of a post-electoral PS-PAN 'contraption' also entered the campaign, with the leader of PAN not rejecting that possibility (Vasconcelos 2019).

On 25 September 2011, days before the election, the campaign abruptly shifted away from this debate when the public prosecutor's office brought charges against the former Defence minister of the Costa government for an alleged cover-up in a scandal involving the robbery and subsequent recovery of weapons from a military base in 2017. While this story lost traction in the last four days of the campaign, it is likely to have derailed any prospect of an absolute Socialist majority.

The election results

The Socialist Party emerged as the leading party, albeit with relatively modest electoral gains: an increase of four percentage points, from 32 per cent in 2015 to 36 per cent in 2019 (Table 1). This increase accrued an additional 22 seats for the PS, leaving it with 108 seats, eight short of a majority in Portugal's 230-strong parliament. Nevertheless, the PS fared better than its contraption partners. The BE saw its vote share decline marginally, though it held its 19

Table 1. Results of the 2019 Portuguese election in comparison with 2015.

Party	Votes (%)	Votes in 2015 (%)	Vote share change 2019–2015 (percentage points)	Seat change (N, 2019–2015)
PS	36.3	32.4	4.0	+22
PSD	27.8	(31.0)	−3.2	−10
BE	9.5	10.2	−0.7	
PCP	6.3	8.3	−1.9	−5
CDS-PP	4.2	(7.6)	−3.4	−13
PAN	3.3	1.4	1.9	+3
Chega	1.3			+1
IL	1.3			+1
Livre	1.1	0.7	0.4	+1
Other	4.0	5.8	−1.8	
Blank/Null	4.9	3.7	1.1	
Turnout	48.6	57.0	7.3	

In 2015 the two centre-right parties ran on a joint list. The individual votes shares of PSD and CDS are calculated by splitting the votes of this alliance in a 4:1 ratio, following the practice adopted in the literature (see, for instance, Jalali and Lobo 2006). In accordance with the usual practice in Portugal, data on the percentage of votes include invalid and blank votes in the total.

Key to table: PS: Partido Socialista; PSD: Partido Social Democrata; BE: Bloco de Esquerda; PCP: Partido Comunista Português; CDS-PP: Centro Democrático Social-Partido Popular; PAN: Pessoas-Animais-Natureza; IL: Iniciativa Liberal.

parliamentary seats, while the PCP had its worst result since democratisation, losing almost a third of its seats.

Using data from a 2019 post electoral survey (Lobo et al. 2020), it is possible to analyse vote switching from 2015 (Table 2). The PS benefitted particularly from former PAF voters and 2015 abstainers. However, these gains were mitigated by the loss of some 15 per cent of its 2015 voters to abstention, thus accounting for the modest overall gains. The BE captured some 2015 abstainers and PCP voters, but was also penalised by abstention, with almost one in five of its 2015 voters forgoing the 2019 election. As for the PCP, while it was able to retain the bulk of its 2015 electorate (four in five voters), it was unable to compensate for the voters it lost (to BE, mostly, but also to PS and even CH), thus resulting in its declining vote share.

The election also signalled heavy defeats for the two right-wing parliamentary parties. In terms of vote share, the PSD had its lowest result in over three

Table 2. Vote switching between the 2015 and 2019 Portuguese elections.

							2019					
		BE	CDS-PP	PCP	CH	IL	LIVRE	PS	PSD	PAN	Blank/null	Abstention
2015	PS	0.9	0.3	0.6	0.9	-	0.3	79.5	0.9	-	0.9	14.9
	BE	71.4	–	3.6	-	-	-	1.8	1.8	-	-	19.6
	PAF	-	3.9	-	2	1.3	1.3	7.2	69.1	2	-	11.8
	PAN	-	-	-	6.66	-	-	6.7	6.7	46.7	-	33.3
	PCP	10.9	-	81.3	3.1	-	-	4.7	-	-	-	-
	Abstention	2.6		1.2	0.4		0.6	8.2	3.8	0.4	2	73.3
	Blank/null	-	-	-	4.3	-	-	8.7	17.4	-	56.5	13.0

N = 1500 respondents.
Source: Authors' own elaboration based on data from the 2019 Portuguese Electoral Study (Lobo et al. 2020).
Note: Blank spaces indicate no reported voting change or abstention from 2015 to 2019.

decades and the third worst since democratisation. For the CDS-PP, it was even more calamitous, with the lowest vote share ever and the party losing over two-thirds of its previous 18 seats. The PSD did a better job than the CDS-PP in retaining their combined 2015 voters. More than two thirds (69 per cent) of those who voted PAF in 2015 stuck with the PSD in 2019. As for the CDS-PP, more 2015 PAF voters chose to vote Socialist than to vote for the CDS-PP.

Besides the PS, the only other parliamentary party to improve its vote share was PAN, quadrupling its representation in parliament and increasing its overall vote share from 1.4 per cent to 3.3 per cent. These gains were largely drawn from former PAF voters, though Table 2 also highlights the considerably more mutable electorate of PAN when compared to the other parliamentary parties.

The 2019 election also saw a record number of parties winning seats. Until the 2015 election, this number had oscillated between four (1983–1985, 1995–1999) and five (since 1999 with BE, and in periods prior to that with three different and subsequently extinct parties). PAN's election in 2015 increased this number to six. In 2019 it reached nine, with Chega, IL and Livre each winning a single seat. Meanwhile, former prime minister Santana Lopes' hopes were dashed, as Aliança failed to enter parliament.

On the right, Chega and IL both drew most of their support from 2015 PAF voters. However, while IL's vote derived almost solely from PAF, in contrast Chega's support came from a broad spectrum, with former Socialist and Communist voters constituting the second and third largest contributors to its vote. Somewhat surprisingly, Livre also benefitted from disillusioned PAF voters.

While the number of parties in parliament increased considerably, from six to nine, it is important to note that this did not generate a major change in the party system. Out of the 230 MPs elected in 2019, 97 per cent belonged to the five main parties that have monopolised Portuguese politics in the new millennium. Moreover, the two main parties, PS and PSD, emerged stronger

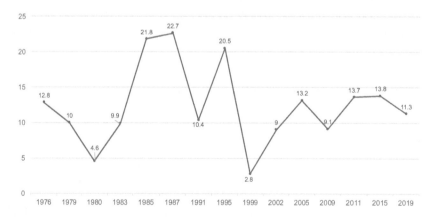

Figure 4. Electoral volatility in Portugal (1976–2019).
Source: Authors' own elaboration of data from the 'Dataset of Electoral Volatility and its internal components in Western Europe' (Emanuele 2015).

in this election than in 2015. Their combined seat share increased from 76 per cent (175 seats) to 81 per cent (187 seats); and their vote share is also estimated to have increased, albeit slightly (0.8 per cent). This is reflected in the effective number of parties: at 2.9, it was unchanged from the preceding two elections and below the 3.1 of 2009. While there was greater movement in the effective number of electoral parties, the increase vis-à-vis 2015 was relatively small, from 4.5 to 4.7.

Likewise, electoral volatility remained stable and even decreased from 13.8 in 2015 to 11.3 in 2019 (Figure 4). Moreover, unlike other countries deeply affected by the eurozone debt crisis (e.g. Greece, Ireland, Italy or Spain), Portugal did not, either during or after this crisis, have a high volatility election signalling an actual or near electoral realignment. The highest volatility in Portugal since 2008 was the 13.8 of 2015, which stands in stark contrast to the peaks in Greece (48.5 in the May 2012 election); Italy (36.7 in 2013); Spain (35.5 in 2015); or Ireland (29.6 in 2011).

Overall, then, party system fragmentation remained relatively stable despite the record number of parliamentary parties. To the extent that there has been a recent turning-point in terms of fragmentation, it took place not in 2019, but a decade earlier. From the 2009 elections onwards there has been a fairly considerable increase in the effective number of electoral parties vis-à-vis the preceding five elections: an average of 4.3 for the 2009–2019 elections compared to 3.1 for the 1987–2005 elections. While the disproportionality of the electoral system prevents this increase at electoral level from fully percolating through to the effective number of parliamentary parties, here too there is an increase: from an average of 2.5 for the 1987–2005 elections to 3.0 in 2009–2019. The entry of CH, IL and Livre into parliament in 2019 (as well as the strengthening of PAN) were more a symptom of the fragmentation that had already started a decade earlier, rather than its cause.

This greater fragmentation came with a weakening of the PS and PSD's hold on the electorate. From 1987 to 2005, the two parties' combined vote had averaged 77.2 per cent in legislative elections and 72.9 per cent in all elections (legislative, local and European) (Jalali 2019a, p. 95). For the 2009–2019 period, this fell to 64.9 per cent for legislative elections and 62.9 per cent across all elections. This weakening of the two centrist parties overall decisively contributed to the 2015–2019 'contraption', by generating the unique parliamentary configuration that led to cooperation between PS, PCP and BE: one where the PSD had the highest number of seats but where the left-wing parties combined had a parliamentary majority. Moreover, the Socialists' quite modest electoral gains in 2019, despite a favourable economy and a shaky PSD, reinforce the notion of a weakened centrist vote.

Finally, the elections had a record low turnout (48.6 per cent), seven percentage points less than 2015. This was the first time turnout fell below 50 per cent in a Portuguese legislative election. However, it should be noted that this drop in the official turnout was primarily caused by a change in Portugal's voter registration rules for citizens residing abroad. Hitherto, these had to actively register in their consulates to become eligible voters. With a legal chance in 2018, they became automatically registered. This increased the total number of eligible voters registered abroad sixfold, from 271,000 voters in 2015 to over 1.6 million in 2019. Given the very high abstention rates among voters registered in the two overseas electoral districts (above 85 per cent since at least 2009), this rule change substantially deflated overall turnout. Indeed, if we look at the results in Portugal, excluding voters residing abroad, the change was much smaller, with turnout dropping from 57 per cent in 2015 to 54.5 per cent in 2019.

At the same time, it should be noted that this increase in overall abstention is the result of the interaction between the legal change noted above and massive emigration during the bailout and post-bailout years. Emigration reached record levels during the bailout years and remained high in the post-bailout period: permanent and temporary emigration from 2011 to 2019 summed over 923,000, of which nearly half (438,000) in the post-bailout years (Pordata 2020). Thus, the drop in turnout in 2019 was caused by the legal change in the voter registration of citizens residing abroad. But the steepness of this drop can be directly attributed to the unprecedented levels of emigration during the bailout and its aftermath.

The end of the 'contraption' as we know it? Government formation

The 2019 results suggested voters' endorsement for a new 'contraption', with a larger majority for the left-wing parties combined. As noted above, pre-election polls indicated that this was the voters' preferred outcome, and it was also António Costa's avowed interpretation of the results (Carvalho & Sousa 2020). However, a repetition of the exact same 'contraption' was a virtual impossibility, with the PCP excluding such a scenario ahead of the elections. Likewise, the prospect of a new but different entente – of the PS with PAN and, if necessary, Livre – was also made unviable by the parliamentary arithmetic, with the three parties still three seats short of a majority.

This left the BE as the remaining possible partner for the Socialists. The two together had a majority in the new parliament, unlike the preceding legislature where the PCP was needed. While both the PS and BE claimed to be willing to renew their 2015 bilateral agreement, this possibility swiftly vanished within days of the election, with both sides blaming each other for the lack of a new agreement.

The new Costa government ended up being a minority Socialist government – again. However, unlike its predecessor, this one did not require the support of the left to reach office. Following convention, President Marcelo Rebelo de Sousa appointed Costa as prime minister. As noted earlier, governments only fail investiture if a motion to reject their programme is tabled and backed by a majority of MPs. No such motion was tabled on the post-2019 Costa government, making its investiture automatic.

Why did new agreements not emerge despite seemingly having popular support? In part, the 'contraption' was a victim of parliamentary arithmetic. As noted elsewhere (Jalali 2019b), in 2015, the cooperation between PS, PCP and BE was the only means for the left-wing parties to defeat a PSD/CDS-PP government that had imposed the austerity measures of the bailout. It was also the only means for Costa to salvage his political career, after failing to win the 2015 elections. Last but not least, then President Cavaco Silva made a written document between the parties a precondition for appointing Costa as prime minister. No such requirements existed in 2019. In addition, while path dependency could have facilitated new agreements on the left after 2019, this was undermined by the weak contract parliamentarism of the 2015–19 legislature. The weak contracts of 2015 made them easier to retract.

Simply put: in 2015, necessity was the mother of the 'contraption'. Four years later, with the PS as the largest party in parliament and thus able to form a minority government without the support of PCP or BE, no such necessity existed. Moreover, as highlighted above, the cooperation between the three parties did not seem to bring them closer together in programmatic terms.

That the 'contraption' did not repeat itself also suggests caution with regard to its replicability in other countries. Indeed, the case of neighbouring Spain after the April 2019 elections illustrates this point. While the PSOE and its leader Pedro Sánchez sought an 'acuerdo a la portuguesa' with Podemos, the latter rejected this option (ElDiario.es 2019), forcing new elections in November 2019 and ultimately a coalition government between the two parties.

At the same time, it should be noted that, while the 'contraption' may be gone, the Portuguese party system has not fully reverted to the ante-'contraption' norm. In particular, the 'contraption' has opened the door for greater cooperation on the left. This is particularly evidenced in the approval of the 2020 state budget, with both the BE and PCP abstaining on the government's proposal. This contrasts with the pre-'contraption' budgets of PS minority governments, when the BE and PCP invariably voted against and the Socialists sought support from the right. Of course, it is too early to tell how this will develop in the future, and its evolution will depend on a number of factors, not least future leaderships on the left and the electoral fortunes of parties new and old on both the left and the right. Nevertheless, the 'contraption' experiment has, at least for now, forced the parties on the left to countenance a degree of cooperation that seemed hitherto impossible. While the 'contraption' may be buried, its legacy looms in the 2019 legislature.

Conclusion

The aggregate voting pattern in the 2019 legislative election bears out Portugal's exceptionality in the South European context. The two main parties, PS and PSD, maintained their dominance within the party, increasing their combined vote and seat share from 2015. The effective number of parliamentary parties remained low and identical to the 2015 and 2011 elections.

A comparison of the 2019 elections with the pre-bailout elections of a decade earlier confirms this stability. There is a decrease in the effective number of parliamentary parties (from 3.1 in the 2009 elections to 2.9 in 2019), despite a mitigated increase in the effective number of electoral parties (from 4.1 to 4.7). As for the two main parties, their combined seat share increases (from 178 seats in 2009 to 187 in 2019), while their vote share remains practically unaltered.

However, this is not to say that the Portuguese party system has remained unchanged. The 2019 election took place in the shadow of an unprecedented post-bailout cooperation between PS, PCP and BE. As this article notes, this cooperation, which became known as the 'contraption', was facilitated by a relative electoral weakening of the two main parties that was already visible in 2009, with their combined vote share since that election averaging some 12 percentage points below the 1987–2005 period. While not large enough to signify an electoral earthquake or a major reconfiguration of the party system, this decline facilitated the unique parliamentary configuration of 2015 that led to the unprecedented cooperation between PS, PCP and BE.

While the 2019 election results suggested reinforced public support for cooperation on the left, the 'contraption' was not re-established in the ensuing legislature. We identify three factors for this. First, while the 2015–19 legislature constituted an instance of contract parliamentarism (cf. Fernandes, Magalhães & Santana-Pereira 2018), it also exemplified how not all contract parliamentarisms are alike. A contribution of this article is the seeming distinction between *weak* and *strong* contract parliamentarism, with the 2015–2019 'contraption' being the former. Its weak nature made the 'contraption contracts' easier to retract in 2019 and diminished potential path dependencies. Second, despite apparent popular support for cooperation on the left, the electoral strengthening of the left, and particularly of the PS, in 2019 vis-à-vis 2015 made deals between the left-wing parties less necessary, highlighting how the 'contraption' had depended on a very particular parliamentary arithmetic. The third factor was the enduring positional differences between PS, PCP and BE, with the 'contraption' experience not generating greater policy rapprochement in these parties' 2019 electoral manifestos, either overall or in the key policy area of the economy.

At the same time, the shadow of the 'contraption' remains in the party system, both on the left and on the right. Regarding the former, the early period of the post-2019 legislature shows a level of cooperation between PS, PCP and BE that, while falling quite short of the 'contraption', has also not fully regressed to the pre-contraption pattern. As for the latter, the parliamentary breakthrough of two new parties on the right in 2019, CH and IL, can be traced to the unprecedented cooperation on the left. By removing the PSD/CDS-PP government and moving the subsequent government's position leftwards, the 'contraption' not only facilitated the departure of CH's founder from the PSD, but also opened a political space on the right that would have been largely undercut with the PSD/CDS-PP in office. Indeed, the 'contraption' also likely contributed to the entry of the third parliamentary newcomer in these elections, the left-libertarian Livre, whose key founding political platform was precisely the need for cooperation between the parties on the left.

While a record number of parties entered parliament in 2019, these elections do not show a fragmented party system. As noted above, the effective number of electoral and parliamentary parties remain similar to 2015, if not earlier. Likewise, electoral volatility is stable, at a level that is similar to the average of the 1990s and early 2000s (and below the 1980s). Unlike other countries highly affected by the eurozone debt crisis, Portugal did not have a high volatility (near) realignment election during or after the bailout.

However, we should also note that politics is dynamic. Entering parliament provides a significant platform to new challengers. The previous two new entrants – BE in 1999, PAN in 2015 – were both able subsequently to leverage this into greater electoral gains. If this pattern repeats itself again, 2019 may portend greater fragmentation to come.

Notes

1. Prior to 2015, only one motion to reject was approved, forcing the dismissal of the non-partisan 'government of presidential inspiration' of Nobre da Costa in 1978, during President Eanes' ill-fated attempt at greater presidential control of government in 1978-79.
2. Google Trends analysis of 'contraption' government (governo geringonça) compared to 'contraption' parliament (geringonça parliament), 'contraption' left (geringonça esquerda), 'contraption' deals (acordos geringonça) for the period between the 2015 legislative election and the eve of the 2019 legislative election shows that 'contraption government' far exceeds all the other terms combined in terms of popularity.
3. While we do find five references to the 'geringonça' by the PCP, these were all occasions in which its MPs were objecting to the usage of the term by the PSD and CDS.
4. The PS also signed a 'joint position' with PEV (Partido Ecologistas 'Os Verdes' – The Greens). Throughout its history, PEV has contested elections in pre-electoral alliances with the PCP. While it has a separate parliamentary group, the de facto separation between PCP and PEV is, at best, questionable (Teixeira 2011). We thus do not include the Greens in the analysis of this article. It should also be noted that parliamentary arithmetic made PEV's support for the Costa government superfluous.
5. In economic terms, the party's thin-centred populism was attached to a strongly free market perspective, with its programme defending the end of public education and health, but this was underplayed in the party's campaign.

6. Wordfish is based on the 'bag-of-words' approach. Its algorithm thus assumes that the relative frequencies of specific words provides manifestations of latent concepts to be estimated. As such, the interpretation of results requires looking at actors' relative positions instead of the absolute positions on the generated scale. Since Wordfish analyses word frequencies instead of ideas or arguments, the estimates produced by the method can differ from other methods such as expert surveys and/or manual content analysis of the documents.

7. To do this, we applied Wordfish to the specific sections of the parties' manifestos dealing with the economy and the European Union in 2015 and 2019. The pages in which these sections can be found are the following. Economy: BE (2015, pp. 3-13); BE (2019, pp. 29-59); CDS-PP (2019, pp. 23-40, 98-136); PAF (2015, pp. 51-92); PAN (2015, pp. 131-154); PAN (2019, pp. 90-118); PCP (2015, pp. 5-48, 83); PCP (2019, pp. 9-48, 57-67); PS (2015, pp. 11-23); PS (2019, pp. 4-18); PSD (2019, pp. 31-40, 115-122). EU: BE (2015, pp. 3-4); BE (2019, pp. 122-123); CDS-PP (2019, pp. 192-193); PAF (2015, pp.144-146); PAN (2019, pp. 143-145); PCP (2015, pp. 79-80); PCP (2019, pp. 107-109); PS (2015, pp. 19-21); PS (2019, pp. 14, 48-50); PSD (2019, pp. 9-10).

Acknowledgments

The authors would like to thank Michelle Macêdo for assistance in data collection.

Disclosure statement

No potential conflict of interest was reported by the author(s).

Funding

This research was supported by the Research Project 'Changing European Elections: The impact of Eurozone bailouts on European Parliament election campaigns', funded by the National Foundation for Science and Technology (FCT) (PTDC/IVC-CPO/3481/2014); and by the Operational Programme 'Competitiveness and Internationalization' (COMPETE 2020) and Lisbon Regional Operational Programme (POCI-01-0145-FEDER-016887). It was also supported by the Research Project 'Into the Secret Garden of Portuguese politics: parliamentary candidate selection in Portugal, 1976-2015' also financed by the FCT (PTDC/CPO-CPO/30296/2017).

ORCID

Carlos Jalali (iD) http://orcid.org/0000-0002-1246-7391
João Moniz (iD) http://orcid.org/0000-0002-5523-6817
Patrícia Silva (iD) http://orcid.org/0000-0002-7044-2723

References

Bale, T. & Bergman, T. (2006) 'Captives no longer, but servants still? Contract parliamentarism and the new minority governance in Sweden and New Zealand', *Government and Opposition*, vol. 41, no. 3, pp. 422–449.

BE (2015) 'Manifesto eleitoral', available online at: http://www.bloco.org/media/manifestole gislativas2015.pdf

BE (2019) 'Programa eleitoral 2019-2023', available online at: https://programa2019.bloco. org/images/programa-sem-fotos.pdf

Bruckert, E. (2017) 'Au Portugal, Benoît Hamon rêve d'union de la gauche', 19 February, *Le Point*, available online at: https://www.lepoint.fr/presidentielle/au-portugal-benoit-hamon -reve-d-union-de-la-gauche-19-02-2017-2105870_3121.php#

Carvalho, M. & Sousa, T. (2020) 'A existência de um Estado social não é uma despesa, mas uma condição de sucesso', 8 March, *Público*, available online at: https://www.publico.pt/ 2020/03/08/politica/noticia/existencia-estado-social-nao-despesa-condicao-sucesso -1906836

CDS-PP (2019) 'Programa eleitoral legislativas 2019', available online at: https://ephemerajpp. com/wp-content/uploads/2019/08/programaeleitoral_legislativascds19.pdf

Cheibub, J. A., Martin, S. & Rasch, B. E. (2015) 'Government selection and executive powers: constitutional design in parliamentary democracies', *West European Politics*, vol. 38, no. 5, pp. 969–996.

Correio da Manhã. (2018) '"Queremos ser o primeiro partido da direita", diz Assunção Cristas', 10 March, available online at: https://www.cmjornal.pt/politica/detalhe/cristas-promete-listas-proprias-e-muito-trabalho-para-o-cds

Cunha, M. L. & Matos, V. (2019) 'Assunção Cristas: "Dizer que sou a líder da oposição é factual"', 15 February, *Expresso*, available online at: https://expresso.pt/dossies/diario/2019-02-15-Assuncao-Cristas-Dizer-que-sou-a-lider-da-oposicao-e-factual-1

Del Barrio, J. M. (2019) 'André Ventura, el ultraderechista portugués', 16 December, *El País*, available online at: https://elpais.com/internacional/2019/12/12/actualidad/1576187485_ 020229.html

Diário de Notícias. (2018) 'André Ventura está a recolher assinaturas para congresso extraordinário do PSD', 2 September, available online at: https://www.dn.pt/poder/autarca-andre-ventura-esta-a-recolher-assinaturas-para-congresso-extraordinario-do-psd-9895497.html

Dinis, D. & Matos, V. (2019) 'Entrevista a António Costa: 'Um PS fraco e um BE forte significa a ingovernabilidade', 23 August, *Expresso*, available online at: https://expresso.pt/politica/2019-08-23-Entrevista-a-Antonio-Costa-Um-PS-fraco-e-um-BE-forte-significa-a-ingovernabilidade

Eco (2019) 'Se o PS ficar de mãos livres corremos o risco do retrocesso', alerta Jerónimo de Sousa', 11 September, available online at: https://eco.sapo.pt/2019/09/11/se-o-ps-ficar-de-maos-livres-corremos-o-risco-do-retrocesso-alerta-jeronimo-de-sousa/

Economist (2018) 'Social democracy is floundering everywhere in Europe, except Portugal', 14 April, available online at: https://www.economist.com/europe/2018/04/14/social-democracy-is-floundering-everywhere-in-europe-except-portugal

ElDiario.es (2019) 'Unidas Podemos advierte al PSOE de que si insiste en un gobierno "a la portuguesa", la investidura "volverá a fracasar"', 2 August, available online at: https://www.eldiario.es/politica/podemos-advierte-psoe-portuguesa-investidura_1_1411038.html

Emanuele, V. (2015) 'Dataset of electoral volatility and its internal components in Western Europe (1945-2015)', Italian Center for Electoral Studies, Rome, available online at: https://datorium.gesis.org/xmlui/handle/10.7802/1112.

Eurostat (2020a) 'Real GDP growth rate – volume: percentage change on previous year', available online at: https://ec.europa.eu/eurostat/tgm/table.do?tab=table&init=1&language=en&pcode=tec00115&plugin=1

Eurostat (2020b) 'Harmonised unemployment rates (per cent) – monthly data', available online at: https://ec.europa.eu/eurostat/tgm/table.do?tab=table&init=1&language=en&pcode=teilm020&plugin=1

Eurostat (2020c) 'Government deficit/surplus, debt and associated data', available online at: http://appsso.eurostat.ec.europa.eu/nui/submitViewTableAction.do

Expresso (2016) 'As 20 melhores frases sobre a geringonça', 10 November, available online at: https://expresso.pt/politica/2016-11-10-As-20-melhores-frases-sobre-a-geringonca

Expresso (2019) 'Jerónimo de Sousa insiste que Governo é do PS e não das esquerdas', 24 February, available online at: https://expresso.pt/politica/2019-02-24-Jeronimo-de-Sousa-insiste-que-Governo-e-do-PS-e-nao-das-esquerdas

Fernandes, J. M., Magalhães, P. C. & Santana-Pereira, J. (2018) 'Portugal's leftist government: from sick man to poster boy?', *South European Society and Politics*, vol. 23, no. 4, pp. 503–524.

Henriques, J. P. (2019) 'O Bloco de Esquerda estará num Governo quando tiver os votos suficientes para isso', 29 August, *Diário de Notícias*, available online at: https://www.dn.pt/poder/catarina-martins-na-tvi-se-calhar-o-defice-real-e-bem-maior-do-que-aquele-que-esta-nas-contas-11250986.html

Jalali, C. (2006) 'The woes of being in opposition: the PSD since 1995', *South European Society & Politics*, vol. 11, no. 3–4, pp. 359–379.

Jalali, C. (2007) *Partidos E Democracia Em Portugal: 1974-2005: Da Revolução Ao Bipartidarismo*, Imprensa de Ciências Sociais, Lisbon.

Jalali, C. (2019a) 'The times (may) be-a-changin'? The Portuguese party system in the twenty-first century', in *Party System Change, the European Crisis and the State of Democracy*, ed. M. Lisi, Routledge, Abingdon, pp. 213–230.

Jalali, C. (2019b) 'The Portuguese party system: evolution in continuity?', in *Political Institutions and Democracy in Portugal: Assessing the Impact of the Eurocrisis*, eds A. C. Pinto & C. P. Teixeira, Palgrave Macmillan, London, pp. 77–99.

Jalali, C. & Lobo, M. C. (2006) 'The trials of a socialist government: right-wing victories in local and presidential elections in Portugal, 2005-2006', *South European Society & Politics*, vol. 2, no. 2, pp. 287–299.

Lobo, M. C. & Magalhães, P. (2004) 'The Portuguese socialists and the third way', in *Social Democratic Party Policies in Contemporary Europe*, eds G. Bonoli & M. Powell, Routledge, London, pp. 83–101.

Lobo, M. C., Magalhães, P., Santo, A. E., Jalali, C., Silva, P., Costa, P., Pereira, M. M., Silva, S. S. & Cabrita, L. (2020). *Estudo Eleitoral Português 2019*, Arquivo Português de Informação Social, Lisbon, available online at: https://dados.rcaap.pt/handle/10400.20/2080

Lobo, M. C. & Pannico, R. (2020) 'Increased economic salience or blurring of responsibility? Economic voting during the great recession', *Electoral Studies*, vol. 65, no. 5, pp. 102–141.

Lopes, M. (2019) 'Jerónimo recusa nova "geringonça" formal e prefere avaliar apoio ao PS "caso a caso"', 9 September, *Público*, available online at: https://www.publico.pt/2019/09/09/politica/noticia/jeronimo-recusa-nova-geringonca-formal-prefere-avaliar-apoio-ps-caso-caso-1885982

March, L. (2012) *Radical Left Parties in Europe*, Routledge, London.

Martins, C. (2017) 'Agora é connosco', *Esquerda.net*, available online at: https://www.esquerda.net/opiniao/agora-e-connosco/46844

Martins, C. (2018) 'Responsabilidade', *Esquerda.net*, available online at: https://www.esquerda.net/opiniao/responsabilidade/56919

Meireles, L., Guerreiro, P. S. & Matos, V. (2019) 'Um PS mais forte é melhor para esta solução política', 11 August, *Expresso*, available online at: https://expresso.pt/politica/2018-08-11-Um-PS-mais-forte-e-melhor-para-esta-solucao-politica

Mendes, M. (2018) 'Notas da semana de Marques Mendes', 4 March, *Jornal de Negócios*, available online at: https://www.jornaldenegocios.pt/opiniao/colunistas/marques-mendes/detalhe/20180304_2120_notas-da-semana-de-marques-mendes

Mudde, C. & Kaltwasser, C. R. (2017) *Populism: A Very Short Introduction*, Oxford University Press, Oxford.

Oliveira, O. L. (2017) 'Eles chegaram. "Não vamos arranjar um nome fofinho, somos liberais"', 29 September, *Sábado*, available online at: https://www.sabado.pt/portugal/politica/detalhe/eles-chegaram-nao-vamos-arranjar-um-nome-fofinho-somos-liberais

PAF (2015) 'Agora Portugal pode mais – programa eleitoral', avaliable online at: https://www.psd.pt/sites/default/files/2020-09/programa-eleitoral-2015.pdf

PAN (2015) 'Eleições Legislativas 2015 – programa eleitoral', available online at: https://manifesto-project.wzb.eu//down/originals/2018-2/35120_2015.pdf

PAN (2019) 'Programa eleitoral do PAN legislativas 2019', available online at: https://pan.com.pt/files/uploads/2019/09/ProgramaPAN_Impressao_Legislastivas2019.pdf

PCP (2015) 'Programa eleitoral do PCP – legislativas 2015', available online at: https://www.pcp.pt/sites/default/files/documentos/programa_eleitoral_pcp_legislativas_2015.pdf

PCP (2019) 'Programa eleitoral do Partido Comunista Português', available online at: https://www.cdu.pt/2019/pdf/programa_eleitoral_pcp.pdf

Pedroso, M. F. (2014) 'António Costa recusa conceito de arco da governação', 30 November, *RTP*, available online at: https://www.rtp.pt/noticias/politica/antonio-costa-recusa-conceito-de-arco-da-governacao_a786263

Pordata (2020) 'Emigrantes: total e por tipo', available online at: https://www.pordata.pt/Portugal/Emigrantes+total+e+por+tipo-21

PS (2015) 'Programa eleitoral do Partido Socialista', available online at: https://www.ps.pt/wp-content/uploads/2016/06/programa_eleitoral-PS-legislativas2015.pdf

PS (2019) 'Fazer ainda mais e melhor – programa eleitoral do Partido Socialista', available online at: https://gabinetedeestudos.ps.pt/wp-content/uploads/2019/09/Programa-Eleitoral-PS-2019.pdf

PS & BE (2015) 'Posição conjunta do Partido Socialista e do Bloco de Esquerda sobre solução política', available online at: http://cdn.impresa.pt/284/9c2/9700333/BE.pdf.

PS & PCP (2015) 'Posição conjunta do Partido Socialista e do Partido Comunista Português sobre solução política', available online at: http://cdn.impresa.pt/14d/378/9700329/PCP.pdf

PSD (2019) 'Programa eleitoral', available online at: https://www.psd.pt/sites/default/files/2020-09/Programa-Eleitoral-2019.pdf

Público (2017) 'Pedro Sánchez elogia a "geringonça" portuguesa de "António Soares"', 16 May, available online at: https://www.publico.pt/2017/05/16/mundo/noticia/pedro-sanchez-elogia-geringonca-de-antonio-soares-1772287

Público (2018) 'Ventura deixará de ser militante do PSD para criar novo partido', 9 October, available online at: https://www.publico.pt/2018/10/09/politica/noticia/ventura-encerra-recolha-de-assinaturas-e-deixara-de-ser-militante-do-psd-para-criar-novo-partido-1846765

RTP (2019) 'Sondagem da Católica. Nova geringonça é cenário preferido dos inquiridos', 1 October, available online at: https://www.rtp.pt/noticias/politica/sondagem-da-catolica-nova-geringonca-e-cenario-preferido-dos-inquiridos_v1176336

Sábado (2018) 'Líder socialista de Itália deseja uma geringonça em toda a Europa', 8 August, available online at: https://www.sabado.pt/portugal/detalhe/lider-socialista-de-italia-deseja-uma-geringonca-em-toda-a-europa

Serra Lopes, I. (2019) *A Geringonça*, Oficina do Livro, Alfragide.

Slapin, J. B. & Proksch, S. (2008) 'A scaling model for estimating time-series party positions from texts', *American Journal of Political Science*, vol. 52, no. 3, pp. 705–722.

Sol (2017) 'André Ventura. "Os ciganos vivem quase exclusivamente de subsídios do Estado"', 17 July, available online at: https://sol.sapo.pt/artigo/572564/andre-ventura-os-ciganos-vivem-quase-exclusivamente-de-subsidios-do-estado

Teixeira, L. H. (2011) *Verdes anos: História do ecologismo em Portugal*, Esfera do Caos, Lisbon.

Valente, L. (2017) 'Holandeses vieram aprender como funciona a "geringonça"', 30 January, *Público*, available online at: https://www.publico.pt/2017/01/30/politica/noticia/holandeses-vieram-aprender-como-funciona-a-geringonca-1760061

Vasconcelos, C. M. (2019) 'PS sem maioria absoluta? "PAN pode fazer a diferença", mas com "acordos escritos"', 26 September, *TSF*, available online at: https://www.tsf.pt/portugal/politica/ps-sem-maioria-absoluta-pan-pode-fazer-a-diferenca-mas-com-acordos-escritos-11341156.html

XXI Governo Constitucional (2015) 'Programa do XXI Governo Constitucional: 2015 – 2019', pp. 1–262, available online at: https://www.portugal.gov.pt/ficheiros-geral/programa-do-governo-pdf.aspx

Index